A POLICE OFFICER AND A GENTLEMAN

A.F. 'MICHAEL' WILCOX

CLIVE EMSLEY

BLUE LAMP
BOOKS

First edition published 2018 (Hardcover)
This edition 2019 (Softcover)

ISBN: 978-1-911273-36-3 (hardcover)
ISBN: 978-1-911273-62-2 (softcover)
ISBN: 978-1-911273-37-0 (ebook)

Published by Blue Lamp Books
www.BlueLampBooks.co.uk

An Imprint of

Mango Books
18 Soho Square
London W1D 3QL

A POLICE OFFICER AND A GENTLEMAN

A.F. 'MICHAEL' WILCOX

For

Susan, Bridget and Stephen

CONTENTS

Chapter Eight: Retirement

A.F. 'Michael' Wilcox Timeline

INTRODUCTION
AND ACKNOWLEDGEMENTS

My mother kept a photograph of a group of Metropolitan Police officers taken in 1941. Most of the men in the photo were auxiliary officers, recognisable by their flat caps, and brought into the police to fill gaps during the war emergency. The young constable seated on the extreme right of the front row is P.C. Ernest ('Ernie') George Emsley, the only one in the row not to have his hands neatly folded, and the only photograph that my mother had of her husband in his police uniform. Two years later he seized the opportunity of transferring to the R.A.F., and in April 1944, serving as a gunner in Bomber Command, he was killed. To Ernie's right in the photograph there is a rugged old sergeant, and to the sergeant's right a young inspector. The young inspector is Albert Wilcox. He disliked the name 'Albert' and, from the mid-1930s at least, he was known to his family and friends as 'Michael' or 'Mike.' Both the Emsleys and the Wilcoxes had copies of this photograph, but until I began this book neither of the two families knew the identity of the man on the other side of the rugged old sergeant who was also, and remains, unknown – at least to us.

While it is not apparent from the photograph, except perhaps in the decision not to overlap his hands, in the family memory Ernie was a bit of a Jack-the-Lad. He constantly teased his in-laws: his mother-in-law by creeping up on her and undoing her apron strings when she was working round her house; his father-in law by borrowing and wearing his trilby, which was much too small for Ernie, and then asking everyone if they liked the pimple on St. Paul's. He was a good sportsman; he had learned all of the dodges, the unofficial 'perks' and probably he would never have risen very far in the police. Michael, in contrast, was on a fast track to senior rank. He had begun his police career as a constable in Bristol, but he had gained entry to the first course at Lord Trenchard's Police College in Hendon and, after a distinguished war record in Italy and Austria, went on to become one of the fore-runners of chief police officer professionalization. His wife recalled him as being stubborn, but he was also modest, quieter and less pushy than some of those who graduated from Trenchard's police college. He appears to have had, or worked towards having, the attributes commonly associated with the archetypal English gentleman. His superiors seem rapidly to have recognised his effectiveness in getting a job done. Yet, if they recognised his abilities and promoted him accordingly, they rarely, if ever, mentioned him in their own autobiographies or in the official accounts that they wrote at the end of a posting. He has no mention in Sir Eric St. Johnston's autobiography *One Policeman's Story* which contains much on the author's role in the Civil Affairs division within which Wilcox served; though St. Johnston himself seems to have had no active role in any of the wartime theatres. The 'Confidential: for official use only' booklet on *Public Safety in Austria* only mentions Wilcox twice: once stating that he was in England when the British Public Safety Officers received permission from the Soviets at the end of July 1945 to enter Vienna, and once in the list of officers that served in Austria. This booklet has the name of J.H. Nott-Bower as the author. Nott-Bower was the head of the British Public Safety Branch for Austria, but he had not served in Civil Affairs during the war and took up the Austrian appointment straight from his position as an Assistant Commissioner at Scotland Yard. Moreover, the booklet seems to have been put together from reports by his immediate subordinates like Wilcox.

It would be wrong to see Wilcox as typical of the police leaders that became established in Britain after 1945, though many of these men had similar backgrounds and had gone through similar experiences. In 1946 Wilcox returned permanently to England as Assistant Chief Constable of Buckinghamshire; six months after taking up this appointment he was encouraged to apply for, and was appointed, Chief Constable of Hertfordshire where he served until his retirement in 1969. Many senior posts in the police after 1945 were filled by graduates of Hendon. There were also a number of men like Wilcox who had served in Civil Affairs and who became Chief Constables after the war. This does not make him typical, but it does make him a model of the ideal of police leadership at a particular moment of British history. Almost certainly, most biographers gain some sort of attachment to and fascination for their subject – even where the fascination is one of horror. With Wilcox I found it the same, though it was a fascination for someone who appears to have been a thoroughly nice person.

This account of Wilcox's life, like most biographies, takes a chronological approach. It is divided into three broad sections and throughout it ties in Wilcox's experiences, his private and public life with the structure and experience of English police during the period. The first section describes his early life, how he came to be a police officer, what drove him to take the examination for Trenchard's college and his experience on the fast track for promotion. Hendon was designed specifically to train leaders for London's Metropolitan Police. It was unpopular in many areas, but given the impact that its graduates were to have on the police after the Second World War, it is surprising how little has been written about it and its achievements.

It is similarly surprising how little has been written about the role of police officers in Civil Affairs during the war. The second section of the book deals with this part of his career. It was the task of Civil Affairs officers to re-establish civil society and services in liberated territories and occupied enemy territories in the wake of a successful assault. There is an official history, but it provides little detail about the men on the ground. The glamour of battles and the men who commanded and fought in battles has tended to delete these men from the history; in some respects they might be considered as the men who follow the Lord Mayor's show to clean up the streets. Wilcox served in Civil Affairs in both Italy and Austria. In Italy he landed during the fighting on the beaches of Salerno, and by the end of the campaign he was responsible for liaising between the Allied Military government and ministers of the Italian government on the subject of police. In Austria he became the chief of the Public Safety Branch in the British Zone of Vienna. The story of the division of Berlin between the four victorious powers is well known; the fact that Austrian and Vienna were divided in a similar way to Germany is something else that has largely been forgotten. As chief of the British Public Safety Branch in the Austrian capital, Wilcox found himself having to negotiate with the Austrian government and also to take up matters, and sometimes having to confront his Soviet counterparts and members of the Red Army. He seems to have acquitted himself well; he was also prepared to stand up to his own Army superiors when he thought that they were in the wrong.

On demobilisation he served, very briefly, as Assistant Chief Constable of Buckinghamshire, and then for 22 years as Chief Constable of Hertfordshire. His time in Herts was one of difficulty and considerable change for the police. During these years, the British Police forces were always under strength, reorganised by government-imposed amalgamations, faced with what the statistics suggested as constantly rising crime, and increasing friction with members of the public, partly because so many of them were becoming car owners and thus coming face-to-face with police-enforced regulations on the roads. Successive governments complicated the issues not only by amalgamations but sometimes by urging technological change as a means of saving money, and on several occasions Wilcox's force, close to London, was chosen as a guinea pig. Wilcox felt for those under his command who got the extra work, but he also took pride in the behaviour of his force and did his best to provide them with decent conditions and opportunities. For about 15 years after his retirement he continued to serve on various official committees and boards; he also seized the opportunity to engage on the fringes of academic life and published a well-received book on the subject of discretion in prosecution. The third part of the book deals with his time in Hertfordshire and afterwards. In the end, like all of us, he found himself having to slow down.

Probably biographers always develop some sort of a fascination for their subject. If not it is difficult to see how they manage to get to the end. I use the word 'fascination' deliberately, since few serious historians can write of some individuals with a 'commitment' or much liking for their topic. With Wilcox, however, I have to confess to getting to like him; some of his contemporaries were great self-publicists and acquired knighthoods and other high honours. He seems to have been a quiet, thoughtful man who got on with the various tasks that were set him and did not tell everyone, particularly those in positions above him, how hard he was working, what a difference he was making and wasn't he just the ideal person to move up a rung to a more senior appointment. He was stubborn, and he had ideas about the police with which I am not sure that I would accept, but then I grew up in a different age. I have never been a police officer, though after some forty years research on police and policing I think that I have some expertise; I am sure that he would have listened politely and told me, also politely, where he thought I was right and where I was wrong.

This book would not, indeed could not, have been written without the kindness of the Wilcox family. I came across a copy of Wilcox's short memoir in the archive of the Hertfordshire Police when I was completing my book on the role of British police officers in founding the S.I.B. and serving in Civil Affairs during the Second World War. I contacted Susan Wilcox requesting permission to quote her father's papers and she sent me some photographs which appeared in the book. Then, rather too late for that book, I was sent other material. The file of papers on Vienna is a wonderful collection of Wilcox's minutes from the Four-Power Public Safety committees, a subject which has scarcely been touched on by British historians or those of other countries involved. Surprisingly, these minutes do not appear in The National Archives at Kew, possibly because the Army or the Foreign Office did not think it worth passing them on, or possibly because some over-enthusiastic weeder assumed that no historian would really want to look at the material or should look at it. It is for this reason that I have not included footnotes – it becomes rather difficult to list, and rather frustrating for readers to follow up uncatalogued material that remain in private hands. I hope that the papers will find a permanent home that other academics can use when the family considers it time. There are, in addition, four wonderful interview tapes made by Ethel Wilcox shortly before her 95th birthday which give a fascinating account of growing up at the beginning of the twentieth century, her life as a school teacher, and her subsequent life left alone with small children during the war and then as a Chief Constable's wife after it. I hope that the family is happy that I have done their parents justice.

I also have to thank some of the usual suspects, in other words those former colleagues still in academic harness who have always found time for me to pose questions or regale them with the latest gem that I have found. In particular, for this book I must thank Paul Lawrence, Annika Mombauer and Chris Williams. I also want to thank Bob Morris, the former head of the Constitutional Department in the Home Office who rather surprised his wife as retirement approached and he told her that he was thinking of doing a Ph.D. I was fortunate enough to be his supervisor. In his early days at the Home Office Bob never knowingly met Wilcox, but he had dealings with several of those mentioned in what follows, including a number that had attended Trenchard's Police College at Hendon as fellow students. My particular thanks to him for setting me right on several matters in his polite Mandarin's fashion.

As ever I want to thank my wife for putting up with me for so many years and for running the family food service, nursing service and taxi service.

But there can only be one group of individuals to whom I can dedicate this book. I believe that they have wanted to see a record of their father's life and career for many years. I hope that this book goes some way towards what they wanted.

CHAPTER 1

MAKING A POLICE OFFICER

Family and Boyhood

Nineteenth-century Bristol was not the prosperous seaport that it had been in the century before. Its profitable slave trade had shifted to Liverpool, and when the trade ended the Merseyside city had maintained its supremacy, not least because of its closeness to the burgeoning textile industries of the north-west. Yet if the glory days had gone, Bristol remained a pleasant centre with elegant buildings and opportunities for men to make good, to prosper, marry and raise families.

In 1844 Joseph Wilcox, a brushmaker, married Elizabeth Clements, a beer retailer. They lived on licensed premises, 'The Sea Horse', where they brought up three sons, John, Frederick and Albert Clements, together with a daughter, Elizabeth. It was not unusual during the period for people to take their mother's name along with that of their father. Albert Clements was the youngest son, born in 1849. At the age of 13 Albert was apprenticed to a brushmaker, his father's trade, for seven years. But the census shows that, when he reached the age of 20, he was serving as a private in the 50th Foot. In the event he decided that army life was not the career for him and, again according to census records, he returned to the trade of brushmaker, but not in Bristol. For more than a quarter of a century he can be found moving around Lancashire and Yorkshire. In 1891, while in Hunslett, Yorkshire, he was living with Annie Dilworth, who called herself Wilcox and who was described on the census as his wife. This, like many working class marriages in the Victorian period, appears to have been a common law marriage. There is, however, a marriage certificate for Albert and Annie from 1900, and Annie appears to have died the following year. It is comforting to think that she was ill and, before her death, in the parlance of the time 'he made an honest woman of her.' Their union was childless. Some five years after Annie's death Albert's elder brother Frederick died. Frederick was a successful brass founder who also rented out eleven houses in Bristol. Albert was his principal beneficiary, acquiring the eleven houses and a legacy of £5,500. In 1906 Albert married for the second time. Ada Elliott, his second wife, was the daughter of a West Riding labourer and only 28-years-old. Thanks to his new money, Albert felt that he could describe himself as a 'gentleman' on the marriage certificate; he also appears to have upgraded his father's trade to 'wine merchant.' The couple moved to Bristol and into Frederick's sizeable, seven-room house at 71 Ashley Hill. In 1911 Albert Clements was describing himself as a 'retired brushmaker.' He also recruited a domestic servant, a girl from a neighbouring orphanage where they received training in service until they reached the age of 18 years. The girl also acted as a nurse for the family children.

Albert and Ada had three children: two daughters, the eldest of who was born in 1907, and a son, Albert Frederick Wilcox, born in April 1909. With his new money and no need to work, old Albert drifted back to The Sea Horse, where he appears frequently to have bought rounds of drinks, often travelling the mile or so home in a taxi and showering the driver with coins as a tip while he was assisted to his front door. Old Albert's exuberance and his repertoire of music hall songs may have been one reason why the family rarely crossed the threshold of their next-door neighbour, the Reverend Frederick Sumner, the local vicar. However in later life 'Bertie', as the young Albert was called by his parents, suspected that other children thought that living next to the vicarage gave the three

Wilcox children an unfair advantage in Sunday School competitions and was one reason why they regularly scooped the prizes. Probably the other children, and the vicar, were unaware of the way that the prizes were rapidly taken to a second-hand bookseller for a few pence.

The First World War had little effect on the family, though the young 'Bertie' was occasionally sent to queue for butter at the local dairy. His mother always ensured that the children ate well; porridge for breakfast and last thing at night, and a Sunday dinner of meat, potatoes and vegetables – maintaining the traditions of her Yorkshire birthplace, this meal was always preceded by Yorkshire pudding in gravy. The war may have had little impact but old Albert's generosity in The Sea Horse was having a deleterious impact on the family's wealth. Shortly after the war's end, the family solicitor warned him that the legacy from his brother was running down rapidly. 'Thereupon,' the young Albert recalled, 'my father gave up drink and never touched alcohol again. This was a remarkable feat of will-power; but it put an end to his gaiety and the remaining five years of his life were subdued and cheerless.' Every Sunday morning the old man also took his son to the paved area close to the city centre known as the Horsefair. This became a meeting place for ex-servicemen and soap-box orators where men expressed bitterness about the promise of a land fit for heroes when it had, in reality, turned out to be a land of unemployment and dole queues. Bertie felt himself becoming as indignant on behalf of the workless man as were the speakers.

At the age of 11 years Bertie took the examination to decide where he should go at the end of his elementary school education. Out of 200 students from his school that gained free places at schools for the next four years, he achieved the tenth place in order of merit. His mother was concerned that they could not afford for him to attend one of the two top schools in the city, fearing that the family had insufficient money for him to keep up with boys whose parents were paying fees, but he was able to attend the notable Fairfield Secondary. However, recognising the increasingly bad state of the family's finances, he resolved to add to the family budget by running errands in the evenings after school. In later life Wilcox confessed that at school he was permanently bewildered by Physics and Chemistry. He coped with Maths and rather liked Latin, though he was frustrated about a system which required that he construe every passage without being able to get on and enjoy the story. He was competent at reading French, and was a compulsive reader of everything in English that he could lay his hands on from Shakespeare to Sexton Blake. Like other children of the period he learned long passages of Shakespeare and of poetry; in later life he found a good, long poem the best way of whiling away the tedium of the car journey from his police headquarters in Hatfield to Whitehall.

The education that Bertie received was designed to prepare students for the possibility of moving on to university. He was a good student. In 1924 he passed seven subjects in the University of Bristol's School Certificate Exam with credits in both French and Mathematics. The principal of his school thought highly of him: 'He is regular and attentive to his lessons, of excellent conduct and is diligent and painstaking ... absolutely trustworthy and conscientious.' But by then Bertie's circumstances had changed. Shortly after Christmas in 1923, his father had died. In spite of his recent abstinence, his brother's legacy had never been restored and old Albert left only £2,100 to his wife and family. At the age of 15 years the young Albert had to leave school and look for a job.

Ada tried hard to find work for her son. She contacted her brother, who had become a successful wool merchant in Bradford. He had little interest in those members of the family that had not been as successful, but he did manage to arrange an interview for Albert with Boots the Chemist in Bristol. Albert recalled an extensive and lively discussion of *The Hound of the Baskervilles* with the representative of Boots, but he heard nothing more about the job. Ada sought the help of a sympathetic neighbour who was the manager for a firm of wine merchants, but he had six children including two sons whose fees he was paying at Bristol Grammar School. He gave Ada a bottle of port, but had no job for Albert. There appeared to be no way of getting a job at the major tobacco merchants W.D. and H.O. Wills, unless you knew someone on the staff. The competition for work in other big firms was fierce, but eventually, by answering applications in local newspapers Albert finally succeeded in getting a post with H. Steadman & Co. Ltd, which described itself as Boot and Legging Manufacturers, Shippers to All Markets. 'All Markets', however, did not seem to extend beyond Wales and Ireland; there were no boots being manufactured and the young Wilcox never saw any leggings. Very quickly his job settled down to nothing more than typing the invoices for shoes delivered to Bristol from factories in Northampton and Kettering and which were to be sent out to shops in Wales and Ireland.

Wilcox considered the packing room where he worked to be Dickensian, and the characters that worked there were as bizarre as some of those that Dickens had created. There was an Irishman in charge of the room who sat alone at his desk, occasionally checking that Wilcox's invoices were correct. Old Bill packed the cartons and disappeared periodically for a quick half pint in a neighbouring pub. Old Bill was constantly engaged in abusive, but good-humoured banter with Fred, whose job was to wheel the packages of shoes to the door for carriers to collect. Among other things Fat Eva pasted Wilcox's invoices on to the cartons; she was unmoved by the crudities of Bill and Fred, indeed she could give as good as she heard. After a while, though a moral teenager with a Sunday School background and preparing for confirmation in the Church of England, Wilcox found himself largely immune to the language.

In later life Wilcox expressed surprise that he made no attempt to find out more about the boot and shoe business when working in it. It could have opened opportunities. Similarly, though fit and physically big - he grew to be 6 foot 4 inches - he never made any attempt to join a sports club. It may have been the family's financial problems that held him back. Ada had to sell the large house on Ashley Hill and relocate to a smaller property in a poorer district; as a consequence Wilcox lost touch with many school friends. When, after two years, his mother was able to move back to Ashley Hill it was to a much smaller property lower down the hill and with no bathroom or inside lavatory. But the school friends, several of whom had gone to university, remained lost to him; he passed his leisure time reading and with occasional visits to the theatre. He also considered where he might go for some more interesting and satisfying employment.

The Sunday morning visits to the Horsefair with his father just after the war and the very obvious economic problems of the early 1920s had given Wilcox considerable sympathy for the unemployed. Nevertheless, when the General Strike was called in 1926, hoping to escape the drudgery of typing invoices and hoping for some adventure Wilcox volunteered as a Special Constable. He was big enough, but since he was only seventeen his application was rejected. This may have sown the seed for joining the police as a career, and when he reached the age of nineteen-and-a-half he decided to put in an application to join the Bristol City Police.

Early Days as a Bobby

An application to join the police had to be accompanied by three references, including one from a man's current employer and another from a magistrate. It was also a requirement for the applications to be verified by a visit from a police inspector, and there was something of a stir when such an officer turned up at H. Steadman & Co. The Reverend Sumner, Wilcox's old neighbour, was happy to testify to his 'high moral character'; he was not aware of the religious doubts that Wilcox had begun to feel even before his confirmation. George Hobbs, a local solicitor, was the third referee; he wrote of knowing Wilcox from birth and, like the others, testified to his honesty and trustworthiness. The minimum age for joining the force was twenty years, but Wilcox was summoned for interview some six months before his birthday. Possibly it was because of his good education. The majority of police recruits came from the unskilled or semi-skilled working class and would not have been educated to his level. Wilcox found no difficulty in coping with the few sums, the short piece of dictation and the general knowledge test presented to him as part of his interview visit. He was selected in spite of being underage but for the six months before his twentieth birthday he had no uniform and was given various odd jobs in the administrative department at the force's headquarters. At the end of those six months he was duly sworn in as a constable by a magistrate, kitted out with his heavy barathea-cloth blue uniform, truncheon, and helmet, and ready to patrol the streets of Bristol.

In terms of structure and accountability there were three kinds of police patrolling the streets in England during the first half of the twentieth century. The Metropolitan Police was the largest, with around 19,000 men during the inter-war period. It was commanded by a commissioner appointed by, and answerable to, the Home Secretary. There was a force in each county which was answerable to a Standing Joint Committee composed of an equal number of magistrates and elected county councillors. In the counties, as in the metropolis, the commander was often a former military officer or a former senior officer from one of the imperial police forces. This suited those in the county elite who felt that their Chief Constable should have the experience of commanding men. It also ensured that the Chief Constable could fit in and mix freely with the county's social elite. In the towns and cities the Chief Constable was sometimes possessed of a similar background to his county equivalent, especially in the largest forces; but the Chief Constable of a city or town was answerable to a local watch committee, a group of local worthies usually appointed from the town council. The watch committees tended to see their police as their town's servants and while there was a sprinkling of army officers or imperial police officers, more often than not the Chief Constable was a self-made man, one who had worked his way up from the lowest rank of police constable.

When Wilcox joined the Bristol Police it was one of the larger urban forces with an establishment of 610 men, and this made it larger than the constabulary of the surrounding county of Gloucestershire which had an establishment of around 450. In keeping with the usual pattern, however, the Chief Constable of Gloucestershire was a former army officer, Major Frederick Stanley-Clarke, while the Bristol City Police was commanded by John H. Watson, a career policeman with almost 40 years' police service and who had climbed from being Chief Constable of Congleton in 1902 with around 10 men under him, to Devonport in 1908 with just under a hundred, and then to Bristol in 1914. Watson was also traditional in the sense that policing appears to have become a family trade; his brother had been appointed as Chief Constable of Preston in 1915. Yet if Watson was a career police officer who had risen from the ranks to command a force bigger than some of those commanded by officers and gentlemen, he appears to have considered that privilege came with responsibility. Early in 1930, shortly after Wilcox joined the force, Watson resigned and the City Council, with some members pressing for the watch committee to be censured, appointed a committee to investigate the Chief Constable's use of policemen for his own benefit. It appeared that he had used an official car and driver for a family tour of Scotland; both he and his daughter had two-seater cars purchased for the police; and he had employed a gardener and had the man listed and paid as a police constable. As in many towns, the fire brigade was part of the police force and Watson had used nine firemen for more than 3,000 hours, to build a garage for his house. Watson's response to the charge was that these were privileges of his job and the same as done elsewhere. This may have been the case, but he declined to name other Chief Constables who had acted similarly. The City Council required him to repay some £1,500. He made great efforts to pay, but in October 1930, with nearly £1,000 still owing, Watson disappeared. His body was found some months later in bushes near his sister's house in Eastbourne. The coroner's jury returned an open verdict, but it appeared that he had cut his own throat.

Watson may well have been right in insisting that he was only doing what senior officers did elsewhere. There were still close to 200 at the end of the First World War, and they were all subject to annual inspections by His Majesty's Inspectors of Constabulary, but these inspections could be formulaic and the different forces still had their own ways of doing things. As a young constable Wilcox remembered the 'awe-inspiring' annual visits of Sir Leonard Dunning, formerly Chief Constable of Liverpool, but, by the late 1920s, a long-serving inspector with responsibility for the south of England:

> Virtually the whole [Bristol] Force was drawn up in ranks on Durdham Downs for inspection by Sir Leonard Dunning dressed in his morning coat, striped trousers and top hat. First the mounted branch was reviewed and dismissed for it would not do to keep the horses standing about. We were all briefed to give correct answers to the questions it was almost certain the inspecting officer would ask. Once that was over Sir Leonard would be entertained to luncheon by the Mayor and members of the Watch Committee. In the afternoon the books and registers and records would be placed in the Chief Constable's office ready for inspection. At four o'clock promptly a tray was taken in with a tea service and walnut cake. It was an immemorial custom to provide H.M. Inspector of Constabulary with walnut cake; nothing else would do.

During the inter-war period the Inspectors were showing increasing interest in some new issues, such as traffic management. But the larger forces particularly still had considerable autonomy in, for example, the organisation of training for new recruits; and such training was often rudimentary. In Bristol, for example, it was fitted around various menial tasks given to recruits, probably because no-one else wanted to do them; and the training was drill mixed with the learning by rote of the definitions of various offences as spelled out in statutes. Wilcox had particular skills, however, and he soon found himself removed from the rest of the recruits and returned to the administrative office, where he was set to work dealing with pay and allowances, ordering supplies and equipment and preparing the weekly reports for the watch committee. When it was decided to establish a police band, Wilcox found himself having to order musical instruments, sheet music and deal with the fees from concerts. Given that the Bristol Fire Brigade was part of the Bristol City Police, Wilcox's administrative duties also extended to that body. He reflected 'somewhat ruefully' that he 'had progressed from invoicing boots and shoes to dealing with fire engines, fire hose, trumpets and trombones.' He was not enjoying the active life that he had expected in the police. Nor were his first regular experiences of an active police life, when they came, the kind of thing for which he had hoped.

For many working-class families the economic situation was far worse in the early 1930s than it had been when Wilcox and his father had gone to see and hear the ex-servicemen in the Horsefair a decade earlier. The new National Government established by Ramsay MacDonald in August 1931, immediately after the fall of his minority Labour Government, aimed at balancing the budget. As a part of this, it set about a reassessment of relief and benefits for the unemployed for more than six months. Local Public Assistance Committees were established to undertake 'household means tests', which took into account every form of income entering a household including pensions, contributions by sons and daughters and even possessions. The 'means test' was hated and it prompted demonstrations in poor areas. The National Unemployed Workers' Movement (N.U.W.M.) was formed to organise and politicise the unemployed. It planned and led hunger marches and campaigns against the 'means test'. Its leaders were mainly communists and successive governments labelled them as revolutionaries, predicting bloodshed and violence as a consequence of their activities; senior police officers appear to have been happy to go along with this. In Bristol, the men stationed in the City Police headquarters were required to act as a reserve division in case of trouble, either patrolling beats for men summoned elsewhere or actively committed to help in the suppression of any disorder. On any day that they might be needed, rather than leaving at the end of a working day the reserve division had to remain on duty until the pubs closed. They were rewarded with a shilling to cover the cost of a meal; men like Wilcox, whose sympathies were with the poor and unemployed, probably did not willingly pass on the information about these payments to anyone but their closest family.

In September 1931 unemployed miners from South Wales marched to Bristol to protest at the T.U.C. Congress being held in the city. The march's leaders persuaded the police cordon at the edge of the city to let them through, but the Congress refused to meet them. Over the following two days tempers reached boiling point; marchers tried to force their way into the Congress and fighting ensued between them, the Congress's stewards and the police. Marchers and their leaders protested about police brutality and assaults in police stations. In February there was another police baton charge against a procession by the N.U.W.M., and a more serious incident the following June when the police set about clearing the streets during a march. Wilcox recalled being told that the marchers in June were smashing windows in Castle Street in the city centre. Police on foot, wielding their batons, had largely cleared the street when mounted police galloped into the action. The number of injured was considerable, partly because the police charge coincided with people leaving the Odeon cinema at the end of a performance and bewildered cinemagoers were caught up in the mêlée. Wilcox wondered whether any order had actually been given to draw batons and disperse the crowd. He also felt that 'it would have enhanced the reputation of the inspector in charge had he accepted responsibility instead of adopting the craven policy so often advised: "Admit nothing and then you cannot be blamed."' When he wrote this some fifty years later, morally he was right but perhaps his faith in what would have happened to the inspector during the early 1930s was a bit naïve.

The Bristol watch committee had originally considered an inquiry into the February events, but then they reversed their decision. The Bristol police seem to have been concerned that there might still be a public inquiry. Yet even more serious events in Liverpool had shown that if a local city government dug its heels in over an inquiry, then the Home Secretary was unlikely to press the issue. City and town police were, after all, constitutionally the concern of the local watch committee and urban government. The events of June appear to have brought an end to the clashes in Bristol when the local Labour Party, no friends to any communists, negotiated a successful 'no violence' deal with the city's unemployed. The deal held, though it was not the end of political agitation and street clashes since, in 1934, the British Union of Fascists began parading on the city's streets. By that time, however, Wilcox had gone.

Wilcox was a bright young man. He did things that most police recruits of the inter-war period did not. He went regularly to the theatre. Bristol had a repertory theatre putting on a different play each week; and it offered a range of plays from classics to those that were once modern and popular, but which are now largely forgotten. At a time when few people travelled abroad he also decided to take his summer holidays in Europe; on the first two occasions he went to France and the third to Germany. He made attempts to learn the languages, he already had a good grasp of French and he took a few lessons in German for his holiday in Düsseldorf. His first French trip elicited surprise from his inspector, who warned him about the difficulty of getting home in an emergency. The trip to Germany brought him face-to-face with Nazi Brownshirts, to whom he took an instant dislike for what he regarded as their general arrogance and the way in which they drove their cars fast, zig-zagging through traffic with the police remaining 'indifferent or perhaps impotent.' His satirical response of a Nazi salute to a Nazi collecting for party funds led to considerable consternation in the English friend that he had made and who was staying with an elderly Jewish professor.

These holidays contributed to a growing frustration about his future in the police. First, like other police officers, he was annoyed by the pay cut of 1932, which was the government's response to recommendation that, because of the economic situation, economies were required in the public sector. In the event the cut was not as severe as had originally been threatened; new constables in their first year were hit hardest with their pay being reduced from 70 shillings a week to 55 shillings; other officers found their wages reduced in two tranches of 5 percent. Wilcox did not doubt that the police headquarters was an improvement on the Boot and Leggings packing room, but he could not see how he was going to get out of the drudgery of administration. In some forces it was possible for a bright, capable young man to get on. Arthur Young, two years older than Wilcox and who, subsequently, was to have a significant role in Wilcox's career, offers a particularly impressive example. Much to his family's disquiet, he left Portsmouth Grammar School at the age of 16 years determined to join the police. He joined the city force in 1925; seven years later he was a detective sergeant and in 1938, aged only 31, he became Chief Constable of Leamington Spa; three years later he was Senior Assistant Chief Constable of Birmingham City Police. In Bristol, in contrast, a man had to wait his turn to get on the promotion ladder. It was not possible to take the exams for promotion to sergeant before serving for five years and, no matter how successful, it was rare that anyone was considered for promotion until he had completed another five years. Since he was not patrolling the streets and making arrests, he rarely had an opportunity to enter a court. During a visit to the local assize court, however, he was impressed with the judge who, after appearing to have nodded off, sprang to life in order to tick off a young barrister and to provide him with a short, blunt statement of what his rambling exposition seemed to be saying. He made enquiries about taking up the law, but a meeting with a barrister who pointed out the need for acceptance and then regular dining at one of the Inns of Court, sitting exams, paying to enter chambers as a pupil and, even then, not being guaranteed a comfortable living rapidly put an end to the whole idea. He sent articles to weekly magazines in the hope of becoming a freelance journalist, but all of his offerings were rejected.

At the beginning of 1934 he was gloomily resolved to stick with the Bristol Police and prepare for his first opportunity to sit the examination for sergeant. He may well have wondered whether it might count against him that, since he had been sworn in as a constable nearly five years earlier, he had never arrested an offender, never reported anyone for a traffic violation and never given evidence in court. But at this point he heard of Lord Trenchard's call for young men to attend his new Metropolitan Police College, which was intended to take the brightest and best who could be future leaders of the police. Wilcox decided to apply, to forget the sergeant's exam and to focus all of his energies on working for the college's open entrance competition.

CHAPTER 2

TRAINING FOR LEADERSHIP

Hendon

From the late nineteenth century the English Police, or perhaps it might be better to speak here of the British Police, liked to think of themselves as unique and as the 'best in the world.' This was a view also expressed by politicians and political commentators. They were delighted by stories of foreign tourists commenting that the British police were wonderful, and even more so when important foreign commentators did the same. In 1908, for example, Dr. Carl Budding wrote a favourable study of British policing on behalf of the *Internationale Kriminalistische Vereinigung*; the Home Office declared his book to be 'accurate ... interesting and satisfactory.' The Bobby was considered in Britain as quite different from the armed, semi-military man patrolling the streets and countryside of continental Europe; but it might well be asked precisely how many British commentators had actually studied the workings and organisation of continental European police. The Bobby was also perceived as different in having no officer class. Following the Victorian ideals of self-help, hard work and dedication, it was claimed that it was possible for a man to rise from the lowest rank of constable to a Chief Constable. Indeed, this had become an article of faith and attributed to Sir Robert Peel when, as Home Secretary, he had established the Metropolitan Police in 1829. The reality, however, was rather different.

It was explained earlier that while an ordinary working-class man could rise from constable to Chief Constable in a town, in the counties it was more likely to find Chief Constables recruited from gentlemen who had worn a uniform and commanded others before becoming senior police officers. The Metropolitan Police, the largest force in the country, was similar. Ever since the time of Peel, the ranks above that of superintendent were filled with gentlemen, and not with men who had joined as constables. During the inter-war years concerns began to be raised in the Home Office about whether the British police were as superior to other forces as tradition asserted. Some foreign commentators had not been as effusive at Budding, notably a young American lawyer, Raymond B. Fosdick, whose *European Police Systems* had appeared in 1915 and who considered that Scotland Yard had been 'passed and outclassed ... by its more scientific and painstaking neighbors across the North Sea.' A little tentatively some were beginning to think that perhaps there were things to be learned elsewhere about professionalization, about traffic control and supervision, about the use of forensics and the skills of the detective. Perhaps also it would be useful to develop a national police college to train men who were to be police leaders in the future.

Towards the end of the 1920s Sir Arthur Dixon, who had overall responsibility for police and policing in the Home Office, drafted a proposal for such a college. Its students were to be drawn from police officers usually under 35 years old who had five years' police service and who had passed the exam to be a sergeant. The plan quickly folded given the opposition of the Police Federation, who feared that it would be divisive and, more importantly, the hostility of local government authorities reluctant to commit any resources to such a plan when money was tight and when the extent of their commitment in the future was unclear.

In 1931, after much persuasion, Lord Trenchard agreed to take up the position of Commissioner of the Metropolitan Police. Trenchard had a formidable reputation as the man who had nurtured the

Royal Air Force during its formative years in the First World War and immediately after. He had now retired and was not particularly eager to take on the management of the police in London; and when he did agree, he was not greatly impressed with what he found. Amongst many of the problems that he highlighted was the way that bright, energetic young men were held in lower ranks through a system of promotion that smacked of 'Buggins' turn.' Trenchard wanted an officer class; he seems to have perceived of the police as a hierarchical organisation akin to the military, and he was keen to have capable, intelligent young men trained to be the officers of the police. Wilcox, who had much to thank him for, believed that he 'never grasped the concept that a policeman is an individual acting on his own authority and using his initiative rather than waiting for orders from a superior officer.'

Trenchard considered himself to be an old man in a hurry. Shortly before drafting his second annual report on the state of the Metropolitan Police, he had lunch with Dixon in a London club. The question of finding good, energetic young officers came up and Dixon's plan appears to have been discussed. When Trenchard's second report was published it suggested, among other reforms, the need to establish 'a clear avenue of fairly rapid promotion for outstanding men... and ...the direct recruitment into officer posts of men who had acquired good educational qualifications.' The report was published on 7 May 1933, and four days later a White Paper appeared containing a series of reform plans including the creation of a college for young men who had the potential to be what Trenchard wanted as future leaders in the police. Unlike Dixon's earlier proposal, however, the college was specifically for the Metropolitan Police and it did not impose requirements such as previous service and passing the examination for sergeant. The entrance examination was to be open to all, whether or not they had served in the Metropolitan Police, any other force, or none at all. This was the opportunity that attracted the frustrated Wilcox in the humdrum of the police headquarters in Bristol; indeed, the six days in London over which the exams and interviews were to be held may, in themselves, have been sufficient enough to tempt him to apply – even if they were in February.

The questions on the exam papers suggest that a good level of education and attainment were expected. F.S. Cocks, the Labour M.P. for Nottingham, Broxtowe, challenged the Home Secretary, Sir John Gilmour, on the suggestion made to candidates opting to take the Modern History Exam that they might consider paying special attention to Frederick the Great, Bismarck and German unification and the ambition of Louis XIV. Did this mean that the government was proposing to introduce Prussianism into the police? Would it not be better to focus on the execution of Charles I, the downfall of the Kaiser and 'the rise of English liberty'? Gilmour responded explaining that the advice of the Civil Service Commissioners had been sought, that the questions were like those set for men seeking admission to the Indian Police Service, that anyone who had studied History at secondary school would be familiar with the topics, and that they were designed to test the candidates' knowledge of European history in relation to British. Cocks was not satisfied, and concluded with the rather silly, if politically point-scoring query as to whether it was intended to have the subjects taught 'by Herr Hitler's agents in London?'

Wilcox himself opted for the examinations on English, History and Maths, although everyone appears to have been required to do specific papers in English and General Knowledge. The General Knowledge paper ranged from culture to current affairs and issues of policing, for example: 'Which four English painters (not living) would you place in a representative exhibition of British Art? Give the characteristics of their work and your reason for including them.' 'Compare Communism and Fascism, pointing out both similarities and differences.' 'Give brief arguments for and against the imposition of a speed limit (a) on private motor cars, (b) on motor omnibuses and heavy lorries.'

Out of the 147 candidates, Wilcox was one of the 46 who chose both French and History; he was also one of only four who were successful in both. Overall he gained sixth place in the examination results, but he got low marks in his interview. In retrospect, he believed his replies had been gauche; he always thought of himself as a poor performer in interviews. He was also aware that his record at games was not good; he had not joined a sports club while working in the boot and leggings warehouse, and while the Bristol Police had played cricket in the summer, during the winter months they had satisfied themselves with skittles.

Within a month, Wilcox received the table of results rapidly and, by the same post, a letter from Colonel G.H.R. Halland, the Commandant of the new college, ordering him to report on 10 May 1934, and giving a list of clothing and sports equipment.

The new college was situated in Hendon, towards the north of London. It had been built as a country club, standing in 60 acres with a golf course, fields for cricket and football pitches, tennis courts and space for other games. There was also a gym and a swimming pool. According to the weekly police trade paper *Police Review*, the facilities and the life for students was to be as good as those available to students at the 'older universities' and at Sandhurst and the R.A.F. College at Cranwell, which Trenchard had also founded.

The College Commandant, Colonel G.H.R. Halland, was a distinguished veteran of the police in Bengal. He had served as an intelligence officer in the Indian Army during the First World War and was loaned to the British authorities as an advisor during the Irish War of Independence. In 1931 he was appointed as Chief Constable of Lincolnshire, and it was from there that he moved to Hendon. His deputy was another old India hand, Superintendent A.F. 'Reggie' Senior, who insisted on wearing his monocle at the same time as his police helmet. Among the rest of the full-time staff was Reginald Morrish, a former detective inspector in the Metropolitan Police who had begun writing text books for budding detectives as well as instructional notes in the *Police Review*. Other Metropolitan Police instructors had been recruited from the recruit training centre at Peel House in Victoria, but since their expertise was with trainee constables it was quickly realised that they were not the best men for the job. Also, since 20 of the 33[1] men accepted as students on the first course came from the Metropolitan Police, they, at least, had heard it all before and quite possibly from these self-same instructors.

The physical training and drill instructors were rather different. Wilcox recalled the sergeant who taught them drill was a former Company Sergeant Major in the King's African Rifles. He insisted that they should learn to march properly in both slow and quick time, particularly on 31 May 1934 when the Prince of Wales flew in – literally – formally to open the college. He also drilled them when, six months later, they were called upon to parade in Whitehall for the wedding of Princess Marina of Greece and Denmark and Prince George, Duke of Kent. Reggie Senior was also there sporting his monocle and police helmet to the ribald comments of the crowd, all of which generated great amusement among Wilcox and his fellow students.

In addition to the college staff, some of whom did little direct teaching, outsiders were brought in for a few courses. Wilcox was particularly stimulated by the lectures of Seward Pearce, who had recently retired as Assistant Director of Public Prosecutions. In place of the usual requirement for police officers to be able to recite, word perfect, the legal definitions of offences, Pearce wanted them to think about the criminal law itself – what made some things criminal, what ought to be criminal? Unfortunately, Pearce only worked at the college during its first term. He was replaced by an ambitious young lawyer, and it did not take long for Wilcox and his classmates to work out that his lectures appeared to have been

---

1   The number of men on the first course is usually given as 32; in fact, 33 men started the course but one dropped out early on, leaving the 32 that graduated. In June 1934, Sir John Gilmour responded to a written question about the students from the Labour M.P. for Walthamstow, Valentine L. McEntee. The response included several errors, most notably the statement that there were 40 men on the course and that none had less than 18 months' police service; it was a key point in Trenchard's scheme that he would take candidates with no police service but the right aptitude and the ability to do well in the entrance exam.

boned up, even copied from a text book the night before he gave them.

During term-time the students were woken by a hand-bell at 6.45 a.m. and, with breaks for lunch and dinner, their time was taken with work or sport until 10.30 p.m. The last 90 minutes were supposed to be devoted to 'prep', either in a college room or a man's study-bedroom. At night-time they took it in turn to act as the beat officer around the college and its vicinity of Hendon and Colindale. What struck Wilcox about the regime was the constant changing of clothes to suit what the timetable required:

> In the morning we wore a blue uniform complete with whistle and chain. After breakfast there was a period of foot drill followed by morning classes, which might mean changing for physical training in the gymnasium. In the afternoon, if we were not playing games, we could wear our college blazers and grey flannel trousers before putting on a dinner jacket for the evening. If we had occasion to go into town it was de rigueur to wear a bowler hat.

The requirement for a dinner jacket, with four dress shirts and patent shoes, gave Labour M.P.s another opportunity to bait Sir John Gilmour and to suggest that the result would be to generate 'snobbery' among the senior police officers.

Sport played a major role in college life. Halland himself was an enthusiastic cricketer who appeared thrilled and even a little overawed when he had the opportunity to invite the chief groundsman at The Oval to advise on the college's cricket pitch. Indeed, Wilcox was tempted to wonder if cricketing ability had swung the selection of one or two of his fellow students; Halland was, after all, one of the three-man interview panel. Wilcox considered his own cricketing skills to be dismal. He thought that he made it into the college soccer team because there was a shortage of players. He also made it into the rugby team, chiefly, he believed, because his height made him valuable in the line out.

After Saturday matches the various teams would travel into central London, headed for Leicester Square and the Brasserie Universelle, generally referred to as the 'Brass Ass.' Wilcox is silent on whether bowler hats were *de rigueur* on these occasions.

In the first term, in keeping with his plans for reform and modernisation, Trenchard had a Metropolitan Police Scientific Laboratory added to the college, though it was not formally opened until 1935. Sir John Gilmour performed the opening ceremony before a cluster of notable guests including the prominent pathologist Sir Bernard Spilsbury. Unfortunately, Sir John was not particularly familiar with the language of the guests' work; Wilcox remembered that he misread his speech and referred throughout to 'forseenic evidence.'

Wilcox himself thought that he would take the opportunity of the end of his first term to learn a new, modern skill – how to drive. The Road Traffic Act of 1934 introduced driving tests which were voluntary for the first year, and possibly in the belief that, just recently, he had taken enough tests, Wilcox set out to learn before the compulsory testing. He consulted one of the college drill sergeants who told him where, for £5, he could hire a bull-nose Morris from a local garage. He spent half an hour with the drill sergeant learning how to start, change gear and stop, and then he left Hendon to drive to Bristol at about 2.00 a.m. one summer morning so as to avoid any traffic. His lack of training and possibly some nervousness meant that he did not change gear until he was out of London and on the Great West Road, which must have been around ten miles. The entire journey of some 120 miles took him eight hours. He spent a fortnight driving around Bristol, before returning to Hendon much faster than he had travelled there. By the end of August 1936 he had got himself sufficiently skilled to pass the Elementary Driving Course of the Metropolitan Police, which enabled him to drive any police vehicle except a van.

Perhaps another reason for Wilcox's wish to drive while he was at Hendon was his desire to keep up with new friends among his fellow students.

Trenchard's idea was to get any able young man regardless of his origins and his educational qualifications, even though, as the entrance exam questions attest, they needed more than a basic elementary education. Some of the students came from good, but ordinary, schools. Others had university degrees; Wilcox was always delighted to have scored more on his History paper in the entrance exam than John Waldron, a Cambridge History graduate who ended his career as Commissioner of the Metropolitan Police. A few came from expensive public schools, had immaculate pedigrees and enjoyed private incomes. Henry Edmund Castleman Lushington, most notably, was heir to the baronetcy of Lushington, South Park, Berkshire.

After his drive to Bristol, Wilcox set off on a holiday to Europe with two fellow students: Herman (known to his friends as 'Graham') Rutherford had a rather similar background to Wilcox, having left Consett Grammar School at the age of 16 years and done various jobs until travelling to London to join the Metropolitan Police in 1928; whereas Arthur Duveen was an old Etonian with a private income. Duveen was the driving force behind the trip; he was keen to try out his new, high performance car. It was while planning the holiday that Wilcox tasted champagne for the first time, courtesy of his well-to-do friend, and perhaps that should have warned him and Rutherford about Duveen's tastes. It was a good holiday, and while they did not make it into Spain, finding the Franco-Spanish border closed because of the unrest, which was to culminate in the Spanish Civil War, they had ten days' swimming in the Mediterranean. The problem was that money meant nothing to Duveen. His two passengers managed to restrain him, but they still returned home with empty pockets.

Much of the press, including initially the *Police Review*, considered the college to be a good idea, though Trenchard's insistence on the men wearing dinner jackets raised a few eyebrows. George Abbiss, however, an Assistant Commissioner at Scotland Yard who had been in charge of police training, strongly disliked the college partly, perhaps, because he himself had risen from the ranks – only the second Assistant Commissioner of the Metropolitan Police ever to have done so. Wilcox believed this was because it appeared something of a threat to the group with which Abbiss had surrounded himself, known as 'the Abbissinians.'

Some Labour politicians were opposed to the college and saw it as spreading a form of militarism within the police. The Police Federation and much of the rank and file were hostile; it was giving posh young gentlemen yet more opportunities. There may well have been something in this, as Wilcox's friend Herman Rutherford took private elocution lessons to lose the County Durham accent which, he feared, was an impediment to his ambition. The college, according to one newspaper forwarded to the *Police Review*, was 'bolting and barring the door to the elementary school boy.'

A year after Wilcox had sat his exam, the *Review* published a leader with veiled criticism of the new college: 'The superior offices of the Force should be the cream of the service. The best cream is that which rises naturally from the milk – not that which is superimposed from without.'

An American Policing Experience

At the end of the course the students were given a month's holiday before undertaking practical work, with the new rank of junior station inspector in the Metropolitan Police. Wilcox decided to spend the bulk of this time travelling in the United States to study their police system. He scraped enough money together for the cheapest return fare to New York. He also wrote to Scotland Yard requesting a letter of introduction to the Commissioner of the New York Police Department. He received no acknowledgement for this letter, but things were too far advanced to pull out and he resolved to press ahead.

Knowing nothing of New York, he asked a fellow traveller where he might find cheap accommodation; unfortunately the cheap accommodation recommended was little more than a dormitory in a boarding house for down-and-outs. The following day he reported to the N.Y.P.D. headquarters, where they were shocked to find the accommodation that he was in. 'A bum's lodging house' was how it was described by the genial Public Relations man assigned to him by the police. The PR man promptly found him a hotel that was within his means, and the next morning Wilcox found himself in a meeting with the First Deputy Commissioner. It turned out that Scotland Yard had contacted the New York Police on his behalf and he was expected; though the New York Police appear to have considered him to be rather more experienced than he was, and possibly older since the rank of inspector there designated a much higher and more experienced officer than a recent graduate of a police college.

Wilcox found himself taken in hand by a Deputy Chief Inspector O'Connell, who showed him round the institution. Very likely because it was all so different from what he had experienced at home, and also because he was observing from above rather than slaving at the bottom, Wilcox was impressed with what he saw. He was also astonished by his own assiduousness in making notes on everything from organisation, recruitment and promotion, to the way that property received by pawnbrokers and second-hand dealers was listed and checked. Scarcely a day went by in the city without a murder and he was delighted to be asked to spend an evening with the Homicide Squad. The squad itself was keen to show him the contents of their car boot with guns, instruments for forcing entry, portable power lights and small forensic kits which enabled them to take fingerprints and test for blood. Unfortunately their efficiency was not much to be seen on the night that he spent with them, since the key to the car boot had been mislaid and consequently Wilcox never saw the equipment. Fortunately, the night of his visit did not require the squad to turn out for an emergency when the locked-away equipment might have been needed.

During his stay Wilcox took the opportunity of visiting the city's Field Office for the F.B.I. It was clear to him that there was rivalry and little love between the police and the F.B.I. The latter were then riding high in the public's estimation following their spectacular successes in shooting down a series of gangsters – John Dillinger, Pretty Boy Floyd and Ma Barker and her son Fred. These glamorous, abstemious, college-educated young men had also driven Bonnie Parker and Clyde Barrow into the firearms of a Texas posse.

The officer in charge of the 90 agents in the New York office persuaded Wilcox to visit the F.B.I. headquarters in Washington and sent a teletype message to advise them of his arrival. In Washington, he was given a tour of the bureau's museum and of the various fingerprints, mugshots and records collected from law enforcement agencies across the United States. He was impressed by the fact that 80 percent of the bureau's recruits were qualified accountants or law graduates, surprised to learning that two weeks out of the 12-week F.B.I. training course were devoted to firing everything from pistols to machine guns; there were also exercises involving firing these weapons from moving cars. In general, Wilcox appears to have been a little bewildered by the importance of firearms and of weapons training to the American police; but then he came from 'the best police in the world', who prided themselves on patrolling without guns. He also became sceptical about the aura of the F.B.I. and recognised how its director, J. Edgar Hoover, had used various forms of media for publicising and mythologizing the bureau. Moreover, while the men were able and dedicated, he thought that they were not all as good as they looked or were painted.

The trip to Washington gave him the opportunity to visit the Metropolitan Police of the American capital, but they seemed rather more determined to get him to a baseball match than to spend time showing him how their 'line-up' worked to enable him to make a comparison with those staged in New York.

After his brief stay in Washington, Wilcox headed back north, but he did not return immediately to New York. On his voyage to the States he had met two young women who had just spent a vacation touring Europe. One of them was particularly insistent that he should visit her family home in Boston. Perhaps she was just keen that he should not miss the sights of their city, or perhaps she saw something else in this tall young man with the quaint English accent. Wilcox himself saw it as an opportunity for visiting another sort of American police institution, the state police of Massachusetts. Unfortunately it was only with some difficulty that he managed to get away from his hostess and her family in order to visit the state police, or state troopers as they were generally known.

As earlier he visited the headquarters, which was in Boston, and was able to absorb comparisons and contrasts with the English system. He was also taken to a troop station at Framingham, about 20 miles from Boston. He found it exhilarating to be driven on a state highway at 60 miles an hour, and informative to hear radio messages being delivered in clear speech. He had been equally surprised by this in New York, where clear speech radio messages were conducted in spite of steel-ribbed skyscrapers and the electrified elevated railway. This easy use of radios confirmed the belief that he had acquired about the extent to which police in Britain were lagging a considerable way behind.

He was rather less concerned to witness some of the other things that the state troopers were keen to show off. The Framingham trooper station had an armoured car and an arsenal of every kind of weapon. When the lieutenant in charge of the post found out that Wilcox had never fired a Thompson sub-machine-gun or a tear-gas pistol, he promptly took him to the firing rage – in the armoured car, of course – and gave him the run of the available weaponry.

Wilcox's return voyage was from New York, and en route to his ship he stopped off to thank Chief Inspector O'Connell for his assistance. O'Connell handed him over to the genial Public Relations Officer who had found him his hotel when he arrived. Fourteen years of prohibition had only ended at the federal level with the 21st Amendment to the Constitution in December 1933. The PR man was keen to take Wilcox to a Broadway Theatre before his boat sailed, though whether it was to see a particular production, or whether it was because the theatre was unique in having a bar, must remain an open question. Wilcox did not recall seeing much in the theatre other than the inside of the bar and, as the evening wore on he began to get anxious about getting on board his liner before it set sail for England. In the end he made it to the docks with time to spare, but there his guide ran into a group of friends about to wish bon voyage to a banker that they all knew. Wilcox was swept on board by the banker's farewell party and remembered little until the following day when, after waking in his third-class cabin, he entered the dining saloon to the surprise of the steward who thought that he had actually missed the boat. The ship's authorities immediately began an enquiry into how Wilcox had managed to embark without being checked aboard. He created a further problem on the following day, when the banker invited him to dine in the first class saloon. At last, Wilcox thought, he could wear the dinner jacket that he had carried from New York to Washington and from Washington to Boston without it seeing the light of day; but the ship's regulations forbade third-class passengers from dining in the first-class saloon. The banker was embarrassed and furious with the Cunard Line; he threatened to create a fuss when he reached London. The ship's purser sought to smooth matters by having Wilcox escorted to the first-class area for pre-lunch cocktails, but the fiercely-enforced class segregation would let him go no further. He spent the remainder of the voyage drafting a 70-page report on the American police system and recommendations on what might be developed from this system for Britain.

Wilcox's report appears to have had some limited circulation within Scotland Yard, though without effect. It seems probable that even if (or perhaps because) he was a product of Hendon, the Metropolitan Police hierarchy would have taken little regard of a recent graduate who had yet to serve on London's streets. Assistant Commissioner Abbiss, whose remit included police buildings, appears to have taken particular offence to Wilcox writing that New York police cells were 'small, dark and badly ventilated, as unfit for detaining unconvicted persons as those in London.' Wilcox's suggestions about police radios, and what might be achieved, moved in the direction that the Metropolitan Police and various local forces were already considering; indeed two years after Wilcox's return, the Chief Constable of Manchester visited Canada and the United States and, as a result, established a radio-equipped 'Crime Information Room.' Even if the Metropolitan Police hierarchy were not prepared publicly to acknowledge or adopt Wilcox's recommendations, they did not object to him writing up some of his experiences for the *Metropolitan Police College Journal*. In 1936 he produced an article on the F.B.I. and another on the American 'line-up' during which arrested persons were put on a flood-lit stage in a darkened hall and questioned by detectives about their identity and record. This was not, he emphasised, to get confessions; only the arresting officers were responsible for interrogating them about the crime for which they had been apprehended. Rather, the line-up was to familiarise other detectives with the features, mannerisms, speech and so on of men and women that might be wanted for other offences. In many respects, this seems to have been a manifestation of the belief in an identifiable criminal class, and Wilcox considered that it would be useful for the English detective who had to rely on the 'slow and haphazard' practice of 'having criminals pointed out to him in the street or in a public house.' That said, however, he found things wrong with aspects of the American practice; the safeguards of Judges' Rules, for example, which were unknown in the United States, would need to be maintained should anything similar be adopted in Britain.

As well as his publications in the college journal, Wilcox further fulfilled his earlier wish to see his work published with articles printed in *The Police Journal*. This reached a larger audience and had been relaunched in a new series at the beginning of 1933, with an introduction from Sir Arthur Dixon stressing that it was intended to concentrate 'on articles dealing with practical problems of police technique or equipment.'

Wilcox's first two articles were submitted when he was still at Hendon and before his visit to America. The first article, 'Detectives in Fiction', fits only in a rather limited fashion with the new concentration of the journal. It was, however, possibly unwittingly, a challenge to the French criminologist Edmond Locard, who in 1910 had established and directed the *Laboratoire de police criminelle* in Lyon. Locard instructed his students to emulate Sherlock Holmes, urging them that every crime leaves a trace. Wilcox criticised the aura of romance that surrounded Holmes and other fictional detectives like Auguste Dupin, Hercule Poirot and Father Brown, particularly for the way in which the stories appeared to denigrate the detective police officer. He emphasised that, while murder predominated in crime fiction, much more often the real police detective had to deal with a variety of other offences. He added that the police detective's work did not stop at the arrest of a suspect; 'If the policeman succeeded in getting a conviction from a judge and jury on the facts which had convinced Sherlock Holmes, he deserved all the commendation he received [from the court].' Wilcox described recent changes, in which the writer Edgar Wallace had played a significant role, that made the police detective appear much more capable and competent. The reminiscences of retired police officers had also contributed to this, even though they had a tendency towards 'touching up their most exciting experiences.' He concluded by suggesting that this gradual change in the fictional representations of the police detective may have increased the public's respect for the police and contributed to what appeared to be a greater sympathy towards police officers than that shown towards teachers during the initial proposals for 'economy cuts' in 1931.

The second article, 'Police and the Press', was directed rather more towards contemporary issues. In the article, Wilcox was critical of what he saw as a modern tendency to regard criminal investigation as some form of secret trade when, in reality, it could benefit immensely from the assistance of both the public and the press. At the same time there were problems with the sensationalism of much of the press which could lead to a handbag snatch on a quiet road being reported under the headline: 'UNKNOWN BANDIT ATTACKS GIRL – RESIDENTS TERRIFIED.' There was an additional problem of journalists trying to play amateur detectives and prejudicing a trial with a sensational story, or else adding two and two and making five. Nevertheless, he believed that press publicity could be of assistance in, for example, presenting useful precautions for householders or warning about forged notes and counterfeit coins. Similarly, the press might advise readers that a stricter enforcement of specific regulations or laws was planned. He stressed the value of press bureaux for different forces, and also expressed his belief in the traditional view of police public relations in Britain: 'Fortunately, the friendly relations prevailing between the police and the public make the work of detectives in this country far easier than abroad.' Wilcox appears to have continued to have faith in this perception of the police in Britain though, as yet, he had very little experience of the police officer's life on the streets.

Learning the Ropes in Bow Street

Although a junior station inspector, Wilcox still had much to learn about a constable's life on the streets. He spent his first three months as a beat constable, followed by a period as a sergeant. He was posted to E Division, working out of Bow Street Police Station. E, the Holborn Division, had five police stations and was one of the smaller divisions, covering roughly one-and-a-half square miles from Holborn in the north to the Embankment in the south, and from Trafalgar Square in the west to Temple Bar and the border of the City of London in the east. Small it may have been, but it was heavily policed, with a complement of 737 men giving the division more men than the entire Bristol City force.

Wilcox was relieved to get such a posting rather than being sent to a suburban or relatively rural district. Night duty from Bow Street was particularly busy when the theatres in The Strand and Drury Lane turned out and people headed for restaurants or hotels. Newspapers were printed at Odhams Press in Long Acre and, as the first editions began to appear around midnight, so printers began to emerge to play cards in the local cafés before signing off at the end of their shift. There was some dead time between roughly 1.00 a.m. and 3.00 a.m. when the agreed half an hour might be taken for refreshments, but sleeping vagrants and down-and-outs needed to be checked as, wrapped in brown paper, they slept on The Embankment's benches, under the arches of Charing Cross Railway Station in Villiers Street, on pavements or, when there was a chill in the air, on the basement grilles of hotels with central heating. By 4.00 a.m. Covent Garden Market was coming to life; fruit and vegetables were unloaded from lorries and vans, and market porters pushed the fresh goods by barrow to stalls and warehouses in Floral Street and Long Acre.

During the first two weeks of his three months' patrolling as a constable, Wilcox accompanied a veteran constable close to retirement; this was the kind of tutelage found in many forces at the time. After that, however, he was on his own. He gained experience of making arrests and giving evidence in court. He also learned when discretion might serve better than making an arrest, particularly when he apprehended a drunken woman who was making a scene in The Strand. Dragging her to the police station he found humiliating, especially when passers-by jeered him; he suspected that the elderly officer who had guided his first two weeks would never have got himself into such a situation.

Some men were nervous of point duty; standing in the middle of busy roads directing traffic. Wilcox rather enjoyed it, especially somewhere particularly busy like the junction of St. Martin's Lane, Long Acre and Cranbourne Street, where the three roads crossed and where, in consequence, the point duty man had to be aware of traffic travelling towards and away from him in six directions. In contrast, however, at the point where Kingsway ran into the curve of Aldwych, there was so little traffic on a Sunday morning that Wilcox thought the point duty constable could be dispensed with. Unfortunately, no-one in authority appears to have considered such a step, presumably assuming that if a constable was required on a weekday, then he must also be required on a Sunday. This seems to have been an example of the kind of thing that had infuriated Trenchard about police leaders – there was a general inability among many senior officers to use their initiative to make changes and improvements.

The fatherly sergeant who was deputed to instruct Wilcox when he put on sergeant's stripes knew how to use his discretion, at least to his own advantage. He took Wilcox into pubs to check that there were no breaches of the licensing laws; he took him into theatres to ensure that no-one was obstructing the gangways or exits. Theatre visits could last a maximum of 15 minutes and neither his instructor, nor Wilcox could work out how to follow a play from start to finish.

The time as a sergeant gave him two opportunities to police rather different crowds from those that he had faced in Bristol protesting about unemployment and the means test. In January 1936 he was in charge of a section positioned where The Aldwych joins The Strand when the body of George V was processed from King's Cross to Westminster Hall, where it was to lie in state. A few days later he left the surroundings of E Division and was stationed in Oxford Street as the funeral procession moved from St. Paul's to Paddington to take the train for Windsor. The crowds were such that Oxford Street became blocked. Hyde Park was closed to prevent an influx of people, and then a new order directed that the gates should be opened to drive people from the obstructed route into the park. Wilcox noted in his memoir: 'order; counter-order; disorder.' The funeral procession was held up for nearly 90 minutes.

Wilcox maintained the working rank of sergeant for his next period of acclimatisation when he acted as a member of the C.I.D. and when it became clear to him that he was not cut out to be a detective. He thought that the ability to observe and to recognise people effectively was greatly over-rated and led to miscarriages of justice, especially when members of the public swore on oath that they recognised a particular individual. He considered that his own powers of observation were sadly lacking. Equally, he felt that his height made him stand out, especially given the fact that Sergeant Wyatt, his C.I.D. mentor, was a good seven inches shorter. In a case involving a woman who complained of being sent anonymous, offensive letters, Wilcox had the bright idea of using the forensic laboratory at Hendon to investigate whether the envelopes had been used before. Wyatt humoured him; but the idea was given short shrift by the Chief Constable in charge of the Metropolitan Police C.I.D., who refused to sanction the expenditure of taxpayers' money on such a hare-brained scheme, and who suggested that they use the traditional practice of house-to-house enquiries.

C.I.D. training took Wilcox back to the theatre, with a return to the use of discretion. Following reports of women attending the Royal Opera House having their clothes ruined by someone throwing acid,

Wilcox and Wyatt were instructed to dress themselves in evening wear and were given tickets for a performance of *Aida*. The first thing that they discovered was the shocking revelation that a glass of whisky in the Opera House bar cost two shillings and sixpence; they thought that they were hardly likely to have such a sum reimbursed as expenses. They took their seats and sat through the first act, at which point Wyatt suggested that if anyone was going to throw acid he would not do so during the performance but would wait until an interval, so the two slipped out to a local pub where the beer was well within their means. They drank through the second act, stepped back inside during the second interval and then, following his earlier reasoning, Wyatt rationalised that they might as well come back during the third interval and when the curtain came down. The pints slipped down pleasantly; fortunately no acid was thrown, and there were no further reports of such an outrage. Wilcox felt that the two of them must have been conspicuous in both their presence and perhaps also in their absence; though it must remain an open question whether anyone was aware of their absence. The important thing was that the authorities assumed that they had done their job, and done it successfully.

Before the end of 1936 Wilcox and his fellow graduates from the first Hendon intake had completed their practical training. They had spent this period together in a hostel in Pembridge Square, a mid-point between Bayswater and Notting Hill, but now they had to find their own lodgings, though with a list provided by the police into whose area the new junior station inspectors were posted. Police officers needed landladies who were prepared to take in men working irregular hours. For Wilcox and his colleagues the break-up was upsetting, but many of them maintained the links forged at Hendon becoming life-long friends and regularly bumping into each other as, together, they became a trained, professional group of civilian police force and wartime leaders. Of the 32 men who passed out of Hendon with Wilcox, two ended their careers as Commissioners of the Metropolitan Police, another was Deputy Commissioner and five were superintendents; another five, including Wilcox, became

Chief Constables, with another one as an assistant Chief Constable. During the war, six served in some branch of Civil Affairs and military government, while another five served as Army Provosts. John Hayes, the prize winner of the first intake, served in both, as a Deputy Provost Marshal from 1943 and through the invasion of north-west Europe, and then as the senior Public Safety Officer for the 1st British Corps in the Allied Military Government of Germany until 1950. The Metropolitan Police was not big enough for him and he resigned in 1951 to take up a post in the Colonial Police Service. Wilcox's travelling companions to Europe had different wars and different police experiences: Arthur Duveen's fascination with cars got him into the Long Range Desert Group; he was then a liaison officer with the French Resistance and captured by the Germans. On repatriation he rejoined the police, but resigned at the beginning of 1948. Herman Rutherford's career continued much like that of Wilcox. He served in Civil Affairs in Italy and, at the end of the war, he became, successively, Chief Constable of Oxfordshire, Lincolnshire and Surrey until his retirement in 1968.

CHAPTER 3

SO MUCH MORE TO LEARN

Policing in London

For six years Wilcox shifted through a range of Metropolitan Police divisions, each of a different size and each with different characteristics. His first posting was to Golders Green Police Station, one of 13 stations in 'S' (or the Hampstead) Division, and also the district where the college at Hendon was situated. The division was much larger than Holborn, covering roughly 87 square miles and with an establishment of 954 men. He found the perfect lodgings with a married couple in Hampstead Garden Suburb; his landlady was even prepared to provide him with a full breakfast when he had to leave at 5.30 a.m. for an early shift.

As an inspector he no longer had to walk the beat; when acting as patrolling inspector, he had to take responsibility for any major incident, and he was given use of a Hillman car. He discovered that he still had much to learn; in particular, he found the need for empathy with the unfortunate, the need to think about how best to treat people in different circumstances, and the common sense that could require bending the rules and regulations to prevent upsetting members of the public or creating difficulties for the police as a whole.

In his first week he had to deal with two suicides, and on each occasion he regretted his foolish lack of thought. In the first instance, an elderly spinster had put her head in the oven and gassed herself. While awaiting the arrival of the doctor to certify death and the cause of death, Wilcox suggested to the woman's distressed sister that she should make a cup of tea. He had completely forgotten that, unable to move the dead sister before the doctor's arrival, her body was still stretched out in the kitchen with her head in the oven. The second suicide involved a servant girl who, driven to despair by an unhappy love affair, had cut her throat with a bread knife. Wilcox took the knife as evidence and then stuck religiously to the regulations, which stated that property seized could only be destroyed with the consent of the owner. He dutifully turned up at the house where the servant had died and, clutching the knife in one hand, he asked the horrified housewife if she wanted it back.

An incident that he believed to have been a third error echoed the incident when he had dragged the drunken woman from The Strand to Bow Street Police Station to the jeers of the passing crowds. Commuters at Golders Green Underground Station complained about a woman newspaper seller thrusting copies of the Communist *Daily Worker* at them. Two earnest plainclothes officers had kept an eye on her and then arrested her for obstruction. Wilcox was called to deal with the charge. The poor, if annoying, woman was of no fixed abode; she could not afford bail and had no-one to stand surety for her.

There was no guarantee that she would turn up in court the following morning, and so Wilcox stuck to the regulations which stated that she should be kept in the police cells overnight. The next morning the local magistrates dismissed the charge of obstruction, which was the cue for the *Daily Worker* to write of police abusing their powers and threatening to sue the Commissioner.

Rather than fighting the case, the Commissioner eventually decided to settle out of court with an *ex gratia* payment of £50. Wilcox could console himself with the fact that he had at least followed the correct procedure, though he also thought that if he had released the woman without a surety, and if she had then not turned up in court, no great harm would have been done. Yet he also recognised that the strict disciplinarian who was his superintendent and who always sought to find fault with graduates of Hendon would have carpeted him.

In contrast, there were elements of the job in Golders Green that considerably pleased him. One of his duties was to enquire into the background of foreign-born people seeking naturalization after a period of residence. A large number of these were German Jews who had escaped from the Nazi regime. They had moved to Golders Green, which had a large Jewish community that took them in and helped them, and Wilcox was impressed by the way in which they worked hard, established themselves and spent carefully so that, within a relatively short period, they were able to repay those that had welcomed and supported them.

What he did not go on to mention is the sad fact that a considerable number of German Jews were swept up by the police among the Germans and Austrians interned as potential enemy aliens in the summer of 1940.

His regular eight-hour shifts gave Wilcox some time for leisure. He began riding at the Finchley Row Riding School. He also took his place in the second row of the divisional rugby team and, much to his amazement, scored a try. And since his Hendon colleague Joe Simpson had succeeded being called to the Bar while serving as a constable, he resolved to reconsider the old aspiration from his Bristol days. Initially, he was concerned that he would not be able to enter Gray's Inn since he had not matriculated at school. Latin was a requirement for the legal profession and he had at least passed this in his School Certificate Examination, even if Caesar's *Gallic Wars* and Virgil's *Aeneid* were of little direct help given the English pronunciation of legal terms from the Latin.

He was also able to secure testimony from Colonel Halland to the effect that he had successfully passed through Hendon College. It was easy to find time to attend the necessary dinners; but rather less easy to cope with the inaudible, and generally unhelpful lectures on recondite aspects of constitutional law given by Sir William Holdsworth, the Vinerian Professor of Law at Oxford.

Wilcox had no desire for anything more than a basic pass, and decided to concentrate on a simple questions-and-answers primer. He was eventually called to the Bar in 1941, when Golders Green was far behind him.

One of the major issues that concerned Trenchard was the rivalry and ill-feeling that existed between the uniformed branch of the police and the C.I.D. Officers in the C.I.D. considered themselves to be the elite, the brains of the service. They tried out ordinary constables for their ranks, and if the man showed some aptitude and ability for the job then he would be appointed as a detective constable. This showing of aptitude rarely meant much more than stopping and questioning characters thought to be suspicious. No-one from the uniformed police, from sergeants and above, was able to transfer. Detectives considered it to be a personal disgrace to be returned to the uniform branch. Trenchard's successor as Commissioner, Sir Philip Game, decided to break with tradition and, much to the annoyance of the C.I.D., decided to appoint some of the Hendon graduates as detective inspectors. Surprisingly, given that after serving in plainclothes out of Bow Street Wilcox did not think that he was suited for the job, he put forward his name to be considered for such a move. His interview with Sir Norman Kendall, the Assistant Commissioner who had responsibility for crime, was, he felt, reminiscent of the interview with the man from Boots the Chemist some 15 years earlier. Possibly having heard of, or even read some of the material that Wilcox had recently published on policing, Kendall offered him a position in the Criminal Record Office at Scotland Yard. Wilcox accepted it, and rapidly regretted it.

It is difficult to know why Wilcox opted for this change. There was a degree of glamour about Scotland Yard and it was an attractive walk to work from his new digs in a Bayswater boarding house through Kensington Gardens, Hyde Park, Green Park and St. James's Park.

He worked regular hours, which enabled him to continue working for his Bar exams and eating the required dinners. He managed to play the occasional game of squash, but there was no rugby team for him to attempt to double his tally of tries. More seriously, almost everyone in the office, from the superintendent in charge downwards, resented his presence. He was both an outsider to the elite and was one of those toffee-nosed products of Hendon.

Yet perhaps most depressing for Wilcox, his duties in the Criminal Record Office were dull and routine, precisely the reason why he had left the headquarters in Bristol. The main task was what was called 'catching thieves on paper', specifically the maintenance of the Modus Operandi Index. The index consisted of half a million cards with the names, aliases, addresses, descriptions and characteristics of known offenders, together with the types of crimes for which they were known and their methods. Information from the index could be supplied to any detective investigating a case and who had little or nothing to go on.

In addition to holding this information, the office prepared and circulated the daily *Police Gazette* to police stations across the country. The *Gazette* gave details of crimes, of wanted persons, missing persons, suspects in custody and property stolen. The office also prepared for police stations a fortnightly *Supplement 'A'*, which gave details, including photographs and right forefinger fingerprints, of half-a-dozen habitual offenders with names, aliases, previous convictions and their usual *modus operandi*. Wilcox attempted to earn his keep by suggesting that photographs of well-known people might be kept and used in conjunction with the material in the *Gazette* so that witnesses might say whether or not a suspect had a look of some well-known individual. He made his own collection of photographs of such personalities which, he suggested, be kept in albums and shown to different eyewitnesses. It was probably not a particularly helpful idea, and it was given short shrift by those superior to him in the office. Feeling frustrated and essentially unwanted, even though it meant losing his detective and plainclothes allowances, Wilcox applied for a transfer back into uniform as soon as he decently could.

From the C.I.D. at Scotland Yard, where he had done scarcely any detective work to interest him and fill his time, Wilcox crossed the Thames to be a uniformed inspector in the East Dulwich Sub-Division. This was part of 'P' (the Catford) Division which, like 'S' Division, covered a vast amount of ground. There were 55 square miles running from Lambeth, south-east to the border with the county of Kent. The division had a compliment of 887 men working out of 12 police stations. In Wilcox's sub-division there was a mixture of respectable working class terrace homes and, sometimes in neighbouring streets, rather grander houses in tree-lined avenues. There were also very desirable districts such as Dulwich Village, which still had something of a village atmosphere with its elegant school, 'Dulwich College', dating back to the seventeenth century, and fine Art Gallery. But there was not the excitement of night-time Bow Street and the rougher areas around the docks and the East End. Constables on night-time beats found different ways of passing dull evenings and long nights. Some simply found a bed in one of the sports pavilions that were to be found in the district.[2] Others found that they could get into a hotel swimming pool in Sydenham; they apparently made so much noise that local residents complained about being kept awake. Wilcox believed that this was remembered when he appeared before a promotion selection board two years later; the chair of the board on that occasion was his old nemesis George Abbiss.

Wartime Policing

Unfortunately for Wilcox, it appears that knowledge of his organisational abilities had preceded him, and as war loomed he was moved from East Dulwich Police Station to the Divisional Headquarters at Catford. Here he was involved with war preparations such as drawing up plans for air-raids and indexing the flood of instructions that poured out of various government offices. It is

---

2   My father, who was killed serving in R.A.F. Bomber Command a few months before I was born, served in 'P' Division. According to my mother, this resting in sports pavilions was a common way for some men to pass their evening and night patrols, although she did not know how they avoided the duty sergeant whose task was to patrol and check where the men were and what they were doing.

unclear whether he was entirely serious, but he also prepared a giant map of the division with coloured pins to mark out ambulance stations, fire stations, the sites of Air Raid Precaution Posts, of anti-aircraft batteries, barrage balloons and water tanks that were to be used in case the water mains were smashed or disrupted.

The day that war broke out Wilcox and everyone else in Catford Police Station gathered round a radio to hear the Prime Minister's broadcast and confirmation that the country was now in a state of war. The broadcast was followed by a few hours of hectic activity which, on occasions, came close to a descent into farce.

An order was received to sound the air-raid siren, but the constable in the telephone room did not know how he was supposed to work the switch and, in consequence, he accidentally sounded the 'All Clear' rather than the warning. Probably not everyone in the country seems to have been aware of the difference and within minutes the police station was surrounded by people seeking shelter from bombs which never came. A uniformed boy scout appeared, saluted the harassed station sergeant and offered his services. The sergeant promptly told him to 'Get to hell out of here.'

Wilcox was still keen to do something other than headquarters administration and, just under a week after the war broke out, a colleague from Hendon came to his rescue. James (Jim) Cole had served as a Special Constable in 1926-27 and had joined the Metropolitan Police in 1927; seven years later he got on to the second Hendon course. In September 1939, after three years in 'G' (Finsbury) Division, he became Sub-Divisional Inspector in Catford. He supported Wilcox's move back to East Dulwich, and Wilcox was off like a shot. Shortly afterwards, Wilcox's domestic arrangements changed.

When he applied to take the examinations for Hendon Wilcox had been worried about his ability to pass the French oral. He joined a class in Clifton run by a Miss Rogman, who considered that his chances of passing were slim; she lent him some gramophone records which he found immensely useful, though whether they were key to him passing remains an open question. The majority of those attending Miss Rogman's classes were young women, who seemed to Wilcox to be more interested in chatting rather than serious study; though this may have been a reflection of the general male attitude towards women in the inter-war period. However, chatty or not, one of these young women caught his eye.

Ethel Edith Wilmot was a couple of years older than Wilcox, and while she may have enjoyed chatting with friends she was a serious career woman. Her father, Ernest Henry Wilmot, was a builder in Bristol; he was a staunch teetotal Methodist, and the father of five children. Her mother, Sophie Marguerite, was part German and a primary school teacher. As a child Ethel had spent a year with relatives in Switzerland to learn French. While Wilcox had pondered his future in the boot and leggings manufactory, Ethel, like her mother, had trained as a primary school teacher. She began her teaching career in the 1920s, took a period away in Germany as an au pair and then more seriously learning German in a boys' school. By the early 1930s she was back in Bristol, teaching at Ashton Gate Primary School; the children were poor, the classes were between 50 and 60, but Ethel boasted that none of the five and six year-olds left her class unable to read.

She later recalled that when she first saw Wilcox at Miss Rogman's she thought that he looked 'a nice healthy-looking chap.' He walked her to her bus stop after every lesson and she promised to buy him some braces if he got into Hendon, which he did; but, not knowing where he lived, she had them delivered to the police station.

Their courtship was somewhat protracted, even by the standards of the time. But then, as Ethel recalled, he was 'not a rusher at things.' She believed it to be the 'competition' that eventually prompted him to come to Bristol to propose at the end of summer in 1939. Even then, it seems to have taken him time to get round to the reason for his visit. They went for a drive in Ethel's car, followed by a long country walk. She finally took him to Bristol Temple Meads railway station for his train back to London and he suggested that they go for a quick walk from the station; it was then, at long last, that he proposed.

Ethel handed in her resignation and left her school in October; they married on 22 December in the Registrar's Office in St. Peter's Hospital, Bristol. Fog enveloped Bristol on the day, making it impossible to take any photographs outside the building. It also made for a difficult drive to the reception at Ubley Warren Farm in the Mendips, where Ernest Wilmot now lived and where, much to Wilcox's surprise, only lemonade was available. The fog still covered everything when they drove back to London two days later with Ethel leaning out of the window to tell him how far he was from the kerb. They were booked into a hotel which they had to find by following the naphtha flares that lit the roads in the foggy gloom.

They stayed in the hotel for about three weeks before moving into a flat on top of Sydenham Hill. The roof of their flat gave them an excellent, relatively safe view of the early air-battles fought over London. One bright afternoon they watched the docks being bombed and that same night they could see the glow of the East End on fire.

'P' Division received its own share of bombs. Sydenham Police Station was hit by a landmine, killing a police officer and eighteen local people. The police worked all hours and even after the Commissioner, worried about their exhaustion, issued a directive that they must have proper rest periods, most of them, Wilcox included, thought that they ought to stay on duty while air-raids were in progress. Indeed, Wilcox thought that a police officer was never off duty, and he acquired his first commendation in December 1940 for showing 'ability and vigilance' in a case of housebreaking when off duty. Unfortunately the comment on the back of his Central record of service gives no further details, but it is possible that the housebreaker was one of those who, allegedly, took advantage of the blackout for their own profit.

The war also meant time-wasting investigations and reports that had to follow up stories of fifth columnists, spies and drops by German parachutists; the latter concerns appear to have been aggravated, or simply generated, by the sight of barrage balloons swaying in the moonlight which had given nervous people the impression of parachutes. So seriously was the prospect of invasion taken that Wilcox, and others, had to learn how to remove the rotor arms from their car engines to deprive invaders of the use of civilian and police transport. Following a government appeal for any weapons to be handed in, he and Jim Cole both acquired colt revolvers in case of invasion or some other serious trouble.

Police officers were usually the first, or at least among the first, agents of officialdom to arrive at the site of houses hit by a stick of bombs. They assisted fire fighters and ambulance crews; and there were other civilians who helped out in whatever way that they could. Ethel could no longer teach as there were strict rules that prevented married women from continuing with the job and there were also restrictions on work by police officers' wives, but she was determined to join her husband in the aftermath of an air-raid. She wanted to see the grim sights of the Blitz and to consider what she might do to help.

Wilcox took her to the bomb-damaged East End, and they also saw the holes in Buckingham Palace that were the result of German bombs. Then he took her to see an anti-aircraft battery on Dulwich Common after dark. The visit coincided with a raid, and the first shots from the guns led Ethel's legs to wobble and give way. Yet rather than dishearten her, these experiences encouraged her to volunteer for part-time duty as a Red Cross nurse at Dulwich Hospital. Here on at least one occasion her grasp of languages – she was fluent in both French and German – was particularly useful. After his plane was shot down, an injured German pilot who had parachuted onto Dulwich Common was brought to the hospital so that his wounds could be seen to. Ethel was the only member of staff who could speak German and she talked to him about his home and family. Other nurses busied themselves cutting the buttons off his tunic for souvenirs.

Even though the war continued, the late summer of 1941 was a relatively pleasant time for Wilcox. The bombing had significantly declined and, more importantly, his first daughter was born. He was called to the Bar at Gray's Inn, though wartime economy meant that the usual dinners were suspended. He also got his first independent command as Sub-Divisional Inspector at Gerald Road in 'B' (Chelsea) Division. The only problem was that he was not allowed to stay in Sydenham since regulations required a man to live in the district where he served. His request for permission to remain in Sydenham while his wife was still nursing their child was peremptorily turned down. Wilcox moved into police quarters in Chelsea, and Ethel and baby Susan moved into a police flat in Chelsea.

Chelsea was the kind of bustling division which Wilcox enjoyed. It was relatively small, just over five square miles, but with a complement of 755 men. It was elongated in shape, stretching along the north bank of the Thames from Chelsea Bridge to Vauxhall Bridge. The northern boundary ran from Knightsbridge to Hyde Park Corner and this was patrolled to the east and north-east by 'A' (Whitehall) Division, and to the north-west by 'F' (Finsbury) Division. There were aristocratic districts with mansions and foreign embassies, and there was Pimlico which ran up to Victoria Railway Station. Pimlico had seen better days, and its once fashionable houses had been converted into seedy boarding houses and brothels. Gerald Road Police Station was the furthest east of the division's five police stations, half a mile south of Victoria Railway Station.

Wilcox found that he had regular visits from the Chief Inspector, but he never stayed for long and virtually all that he did was to sign papers as necessary. Wilcox himself had little occasion to visit his superintendent, except when he needed to apply for warrants to raid brothels or gaming houses. As for the C.I.D., he was happy not to defy convention and to let the detective inspector in the station get on with things.

The war brought new duties for the police, most obviously in the enforcement of defence regulations such as the blackout. Various wartime shortages also fostered a widespread black market that involved many ordinary people buying and selling what were, at the time, little luxuries; at the other end were significant racketeers. While most people were keen to see tough action taken against the latter, occasional small-scale acquisitions, sometimes for a celebration such as a wedding, were rarely seen by the mass of the population as criminal and no doubt many a policeman's wife, and the policeman himself, were not averse to a favour from their neighbourhood butcher or greengrocer. Wilcox's sub-division had an additional way to eke out the food supply. Somehow someone got hold of a pig; it was fed on scraps by individuals in the station, and finally slaughtered with the meat distributed.

The black market required constant investigation, but there were one-off problems, the most serious of which occurred shortly before Christmas 1941. Wilcox was summoned to Scotland Yard and informed that there was the possibility of Spain being pressurised by Germany to let German troops cross Spanish territory in order to attack Gibraltar and then to effect a landing in north-west Africa. Wilcox was directed to have six men, a van and a driver ready at all times to put a cordon round the embassy and to prevent anyone entering or leaving should this eventuality arise. Determined to ensure that he was always on top of the situation, and reluctant to inform his deputy of his top-secret orders, Wilcox remained in the station over Christmas sleeping on a camp bed in an office. There was widespread speculation about the van, its driver and the six policemen who sat playing cards in the canteen awaiting orders. In the event, they were never called into action and when they were stood down no-one was any the wiser, other than Wilcox, a few senior figures at Scotland Yard and a few civil servants.

At around the same time Wilcox found himself having to sort out a problem for a former government minister who really ought to have known better than requesting police assistance. Frederic Herbert Maugham, 1st Viscount Maugham, was a prestigious High Court Judge who had been Neville Chamberlain's Lord Chancellor from 1938-39. He complained to Wilcox about a young woman pestering members of his family. Technically there were legal remedies for this in the civil courts, but Wilcox was reluctant to instruct a former Lord Chancellor in the law. He ordered an elderly sergeant to deal with the problem if the young woman turned up at Maugham's house again. The resulting appearance of the sergeant seems to have been successful, even though initially he had to restrain the woman physically. The police heard nothing more; and if Wilcox ever knew the cause of the young woman's hysterical behaviour, he kept it to himself.

Domestic problems like those of Viscount Maugham and international incidents that threatened over Christmas in 1941 were not usual. The growth of the black market and the need to enforce the blackout and similar regulations were probably seen as an annoying extension of ordinary police duties, even in wartime. Other wartime difficulties for the men of Gerald Road Police Station were the result of their proximity to Victoria Railway Station.

Thousands of servicemen passed through Victoria in transit or on leave. Checking whether soldiers were carrying the right pass, or any pass was the task of the Military Police who, much to the annoyance of ordinary squaddies, patrolled the station and its immediate vicinity. Not all of the Redcaps deserved their unsavoury reputation with the soldiers, but some do appear to have thrown their weight around, especially if they were met with cheek. Men could find themselves vindictively put on a charge for a dirty uniform, boots or equipment, for not having their laces properly tied or their brasses shining. This was not a matter for the patrolling Bobby, unless an altercation brought civilian involvement usually to the side of the squaddie.

But there was a much greater problem for the ordinary policeman resulting from the number of pubs, servicemen's clubs and temporary brothels that sprang up around the railway station.

Pubs and servicemen's clubs presented the traditional police problem of arguments spilling out into the streets and turning into fights. In wartime, with servicemen involved, the numbers taking part could be considerable. Rivalry between different regiments, between different sections of the armed services, and between servicemen from different Allied powers all provided the spur for single clashes or for groups of men to exchange punches.

Brothels were more complicated. Unlike continental Europe, the British had no system for the regular checking of female sex-workers and no registration of brothels; soliciting was an offence, and so too was keeping a brothel – in legal terms 'keeping a disorderly house.' The police knew many regular prostitutes, and there were stories of women being given a degree of licence and being hauled before the magistrate for a fine only when it was 'their turn.'

The prosecution of brothel keepers was much more complex and time-consuming, and the brothel-keepers in Wilcox's sub-division appear to have been householders who let out rooms for the trade. To ensure an arrest and conviction it was necessary to have two experienced officers watching the premises for several nights, making a note of the number of couples admitted, the time that they entered and the time that they left. A superior officer, commonly a sub-divisional officer such as Wilcox, read their paperwork and if he agreed to take it forward, he had to get the permission of the Deputy Assistant Commissioner for authority to mount a raid. Armed with that authority, the sub-divisional officer had to seek the approval of the solicitor of the Westminster County Council; the intention here was to demonstrate that the council were doing their best to prevent property from being used for disorderly purposes. At the same time, a warrant was required from a Bow Street magistrate. And after this rigmarole, the right moment had to be determined for a police raid. The raid itself was almost always at night and lasted at least an hour, as statements were required from the men and women in the house and, finally, the brothel-keeper was formally charged. There followed the writing up of reports and, with very little sleep, the officers responsible for laying any charges had to appear the following morning in Bow Street Magistrates' Court to present their evidence.

The work may have been tiring, but initially Wilcox found it exciting. His enthusiasm for the work, however, led to a problem when some of the brothel-keepers protested that a large hotel in the smart Eccleston Square was doing the same as them but that it was being protected. Wilcox took the complaints to the Deputy Assistant Commissioner, who explained: 'Look here, if we go on like this we shall have to close half the hotels in the West End.' The case went no further and Wilcox began to wonder if, indeed, he was pursuing matters along the right lines. He recognised and understood the concerns of the military authorities about venereal disease and its serious harm to their fighting men; but he also reasoned that it hardly mattered if a young soldier wanted a sexual experience before going overseas to fight and possibly to die.

He also worried about the numbers of young women, some still in their teens, who had gravitated to London and who seemed to be getting swept up into prostitution. At the end of one raid on a house in Pimlico he decided to play matters differently from the usual interviews and arrests. There were 21 American and Canadian soldiers in the house with 21 girls and, instead of the usual practice of letting everyone else go but for the brothel-keeper who was charged, he decided to take to the police station any of the girls that looked to be under the age of 21 and charge them with giving false names and addresses under the wartime Defence Regulations. He and a team of officers then spent the night using the indices at Scotland Yard trying to trace the girls' backgrounds; as a result he found some who had been reported as missing from home and others who had absconded from approved schools.

The following morning Wilcox turned up at Bow Street Magistrates' Court, tired but feeling pleased with himself. The feeling of pleasure and satisfaction, however, did not last long. He found himself confronted by Superintendent Dorothy Peto, the head of the Women's Branch of the Metropolitan Police. The formidable Miss Peto had been an organiser for the British Social Hygiene Council before joining the police, and by the end of the 1930s her policewomen were responsible for most cases involving child abuse and, when available, for interviewing almost all women in London involved in indecency cases.

She had been informed during the night that Wilcox and his men were conducting investigations following a brothel raid and were consulting the missing persons' indices. 'Why,' she wanted to know, 'did you not take a policewoman on the raid with you?'

In the contemporary world she would have been on solid ground, but there was nothing in the law or in the police regulations that required the presence of women police in such circumstances in the inter-war and wartime period. Wilcox did not record his response, but probably he was keen to avoid any awkward confrontation with a superintendent, even if few of his contemporary senior officers would publicly have considered her an equal. Possibly it was this case which, at the end of January 1943, earned him his second commendation, this time for 'good work in connection with proceedings against keepers of a disorderly house.' Wilcox seems to have been too modest to mention his commendations in his short memoir; or perhaps he simply saw both instances a part of a police officer's job and hardly worth the fuss.

Preparing for War Service

At the beginning of the First World War, the police had become seriously undermanned as reservists were recalled to the colours and as large numbers of fit young men left at Kitchener's call to fight for King and Country.

From at least the mid-1930s there were worries that, in the event of a new war, the same problems could arise. Discussions between the War Office and the Home Office resulted in an agreement that reservists would not be recalled until three months after the beginning of any conflict and there was intensive recruitment of special constables and police reserves, often former police officers prepared to serve again if required.

As the war continued, there was also an increase in the number of women police, though many of these were not attested as constables and the few Chief Constables prepared to recruit them rarely considered them as capable of much more than making tea, filing and sitting at a typewriter. The result was that, while police numbers did not decline during the conflict, police forces aged and by 1945 there were men serving who were long past their retirement date.

It was impossible to recruit new men since they were required by the armed services; serving officers could not volunteer for the services except on the few occasions that permission was given. In 1943 there was one such call for men to volunteer as Civil Affairs officers when the British and the Americans believed that it would be necessary for men with specific expertise to move with the armies and to re-establish civil society and reconstruct its needs in liberated and captured territories. Police officers were seen as having a major role to play here, particularly among the British who believed their own claims to having 'the best police in the world.' The Bobby, it was stressed, was a pillar of the British constitutional system and it was, among other things, his quiet authority and his close links with the public that had contributed to Britain's absence of the revolutions that appeared to have plagued nineteenth-century Europe.

This was uncritical, special pleading, but it had a strong appeal especially alongside popular, nationalistic perceptions of incompetent and sometimes brutal Italian police, and cold, menacing German police; in the British mind, every German police officer was a murderous, Gestapo thug.

Wilcox joked that his colt revolver was no longer needed to defend East Dulwich from German invaders, and he jumped at the opportunity offered to volunteer for Civil Affairs. The new organisation gave him the opportunity to do his bit for the war effort, as well as the opportunity for something exciting and different that would keep him away from administration, even more than his position in Gerald Road.

In the provinces, police officers had to get the permission of their watch committee or standing joint committee to proceed. In the Metropolitan Police they had to seek permission from the Commissioner, and nothing and no-one stood in Wilcox's way, not even Ethel with their small daughter and a second child on the way.

Sir Frank Brook, one of His Majesty's Inspectors of Constabulary, was appointed to advise on police matters for Civil Affairs and, with the approval of the Oxfordshire S.J.C., he had their young Chief Constable, Eric St. Johnston, seconded to him full-time to assist with planning.

St. Johnston had a Cambridge degree and had passed through the third course at Hendon as head of the class. He had become Chief Constable of Oxfordshire in 1940. He was far more ambitious and driven than Wilcox and, in his autobiography, he gives himself a rather more significant role in the creation of the police section of Civil Affairs than War Office documentation suggests, for example making a decision that 500 police officers should be trained. The junior officers were to attend a course at the Metropolitan Police training school in Peel House, close to Victoria and Wilcox's Chelsea sub-division. The Commandant here was Arthur Young who, as explained earlier, had risen rapidly without the benefit of Hendon to become Senior Assistant Chief Constable of Birmingham; it was from here that he moved to train junior Civil Affairs Officers at Peel House.

Wilcox, however, was regarded as a senior officer and was sent to be trained at Southlands College in Wimbledon. Southlands had been a Methodist College for women training to be teachers; the young women had been moved to Weston-super-Mare, and the Army moved in.

The atmosphere, the banter and the curriculum all changed significantly when Wilcox and his new comrades arrived at Southlands for instruction in the summer of 1943. There were a few American officers wearing their Olive Drab uniforms, British officers, including it seems some men from different civilian professions and administrative bodies keen to get a uniform and now dressed in battledress or more formal dress with Sam Browne belts, as well as police and fire-brigade men still in their dark blue.

They were given a variety of lectures on the different constitutional, government and police systems to be found across Europe; and a few that drew attention to things such as 'the German mind.'

Many of the lecturers were academics or high-ranking civil servants; at least Wilcox was not as critical of these as he had been of Sir William Holdsworth, who lectured him on civil law at Gray's Inn.

Eric St. Johnston also pitched in with lectures on the aims and principles of Civil Affairs. The group to which Wilcox was attached was directed to make an intensive study of Pas-de-Calais; the implication being that this was where they were to be sent following an invasion of northern Europe. By the end of their month at Southlands, Wilcox reckoned that they knew the French *département* – its topography, economy, local government – intimately. The pity was that they never had occasion to use their detailed work on France, moreover, in spite of their training they were not the first British police officers to land in Europe as members of the Allied Military Government.

The volunteers for Civil Affairs were only beginning their training when it was recognised that they would not be ready for the planned landing in Sicily. As a result there was a rapid chase to find 60 new volunteers from the Metropolitan Police, although some men were encouraged to volunteer before they agreed to step forward.

Gerald Richardson, a Hendon graduate then serving as a Detective Inspector in Harlesden, was one such. He recalled being summoned to a meeting with Sir Norman Kendall wondering what offence he had committed. Rather than tell him off, Kendall simply suggested that he volunteer; and it seems unlikely that Kendall wished to be rid of Richardson, who had served in Limehouse; had been involved in the campaign against I.R.A. bombers and had worked on fraud cases for the War Damage Commission. Another graduate, Frank Rawlings, then serving as an inspector in Lambeth, had attended the same Hendon course as Richardson and was similarly invited to volunteer. Both were in Sicily by the end of July; and with them, as Director of Public Safety, was Arthur Young, who had left Peel House for the field.

Policing was often boring routine, whether patrolling the street or working on administration in a police station; the routine was occasionally enlivened by an incident that required instant decisions and immediate action.

Wilcox and his fellow police officers serving in Civil Affairs soon found that there were similarities with life in the Army. The rush to get men for the invasion of Sicily was a good example of this kind of periodic frenetic action. Yet men were invariably kept in the dark about what was happening and left twiddling their thumbs, waiting until someone, somewhere, made a decision and launched a period of action.

After a few weeks in Wimbledon, he and his comrades were ordered to the Great Eastern Hotel on the Euston Road and to be ready to move from there on twenty-four hours' notice. On several occasions they were ordered to pack and assemble in readiness to move off, and then they were stood down.

Wilcox used the dead time in his final week before embarkation to make several visits to a nursing home in Sydenham to see Ethel and his second daughter, Bridget, who was just a few days old. His last visit was on 10 August 1943. He had lunch with Ethel, and the matron urged him to rest since he must be feeling the results of an armful of jabs for typhus, yellow fever, malaria and smallpox. He could not say that he was about to leave for the war. Nor could he say where he was going; he did not know himself.

That evening, Acting Major Wilcox found himself on a train for Glasgow; the following day he embarked on the S.S. *Ormonde.*

CHAPTER 4

ITALY

First Steps as a Liberator

The S.S. *Ormonde* had been built by Orient Lines as a troopship during the First World War. When peace returned, she had been returned to Orient Lines, sailing the route to Australia via Suez.

In 1939 she was recalled for service as a troopship, and in the third week of August 1943 was one of 18 ships that were assembled as convoy in the Clyde. When the ships, packed with 50,000 men, set sail into the Atlantic they were accompanied by an escort of half-a-dozen corvettes, two light cruisers and an aircraft carrier. A week at sea took them down the western coast of Britain and then the Iberian Peninsula to the Straits of Gibraltar.

The voyage was uneventful, though stories circulated on the *Ormonde* that U-boats had been spotted, very probably just to put the wind up those that were not in on the joke. The convoy passed through the Straits in the dead of night and the men were ordered to change into their tropical kit. A week after leaving the Clyde the convoy received a new escort of American aircraft and it then dropped anchor, under the protection of barrage balloons in the Bay of Algiers.

It was intended that Civil Affairs would have British and American officers interleaved and serving side-by-side. Two days after disembarking from the *Ormonde* in Algiers, Wilcox was summoned to the Hotel Alexandria for an interview with an American General. General Frank J. McSherry was an engineer and veteran of the First World War who had recently been appointed as Deputy Chief of Allied Military Government Europe.

Wilcox thought McSherry 'bluff'; he was certainly blunt. After informing Wilcox that he was to be attached to the U.S. VI Corps, he told him that first and foremost he was always to ensure that the dead were buried promptly as he did not want rotting corpses spreading disease and infection among the troops – a matter that had been neglected in the lectures at Wimbledon.

The aftermath of the interview was brightened when Wilcox bumped into 'Steve' Stephens,[3] an acquaintance from the Wimbledon course. Stephens was ten years older than Wilcox. He had started life as a Boilermaker's Plater in Sheerness Dockyard, joining the Metropolitan Police in 1919. He had not gone to Hendon, but had risen to be a sub-divisional inspector at Brixton in the Lambeth ('L') Division by the middle of 1942.

Shortly after the meeting with McSherry the whole group of Civil Affairs officers, of which Wilcox and Stephens were members, were ordered to climb into two trucks and driven some sixty miles to the east to Tizi Ousou. Wilcox called it a village, though it appears to have been rather larger than that would imply and today it is one of the larger cities in Algeria. It lay close to a wadi in the Great Kabylie mountain region; its name is roughly translated as the '(mountain) gap of Forsythia', which suggests a delightful setting.

They arrived in the dark at a school where they were to be based; no-one was there to meet them and they had to find empty dormitories to put up their beds. The next morning they found that

---

3   Wilcox calls him 'Stevens' but on the list of officers given in Col. Arthur Young's account of the police that served in Italy (TNA WO 220/492) he is 'Stephens'. In the Metropolitan Police Central Records of Service, Dean Frederick William Stephens was born in Kennington in 1897 and joined the police in May 1919. He was demobbed as a major in Civil Affairs in 1945, but was unable to continue his police service owing to chronic dyspepsia.

their training was far from over and a short, fiery Scottish Colonel was determined to get them into what he considered to be the appropriate military shape.

The Americans in the party, generally a few years older than their British counterparts, wanted to smoke their cigars and gamble. They thought the Colonel mad, especially when he ordered them to embark on a route march in the middle of the day. Even though the village had a delightful name, the mean temperature in the middle of the day was anything from the upper-20s centigrade to the mid-30s. Wilcox and Stephens were directed to lead, and having covered around a half mile the whole group took the democratic decision to stop at a hotel and to have a long, cool drink before getting back into some form of order and marching back to the Colonel.

Two Italian language lessons gave them a clue as to where they might be heading, and after three days in Tizi Ousou General McSherry reappeared to inform them that they were about to participate in the invasion of the Italian mainland.

The party returned to Algiers, waited for six hours and then made a night journey through the cold Atlas Mountains, stopping eventually at the small port of Mostaganem. The stop was short, possibly because someone spotted General Eisenhower when they should not have done. They moved further along the coast to a tiny resort called Porte des Poules. Assuming that the stop might, at last, be one of reasonable duration they took the opportunity of a swim in the Mediterranean. However, they were rapidly ordered to repack, remount their trucks and drive another 30 miles to the docks at Oran. There was no stopping here at all; after driving straight into the docks Wilcox and two other British officers – one an official for London Transport, the other from the Borstal Service - were immediately embarked on a Liberty ship, the *James W. Marshall*.

The week of rushing east and west across the Algerian seaboard had been hectic with little awareness of what was happening, where they were going and why. At last, given the ship's cargo, there was some certainty that they were heading for a conflict zone; but most of the G.I.s that embarked on ships alongside Wilcox had, like him, never seen battlefield action and for the men whose task was to take, to hold and then to move forward from the beach at Salerno, the landing was to come as a terrifying shock.

The *James W. Marshall* was one of 40 ships making up a convoy bound for Salerno. Some of the ships flew barrage balloons to inhibit air attacks. The new Italian government may have come to an agreement with the Allies, but there was clumsiness in the negotiations and delays. This meant that there was no Allied landing to take Rome but others in the south, such as Salerno, went ahead. Unfortunately, the Germans found the time to seize Italian airfields; the barrage balloons in the convoy that took Wilcox to Italy were necessary, though not particularly successful in preventing some sporadic air attacks. A rumour circulated on the ship that the skipper, a giant Scandinavian with rudimentary English, was allowed to claim a danger money bonus for each air attack and as a consequence was earning more than Eisenhower.

In addition, conditions on the ship were uncomfortable. The quarters were hot and stuffy. The deck was packed with trucks, landing craft, rafts, petrol and guns. There appears to have been little attempt to maintain much discipline among the G.I. drivers and mechanics who, Wilcox noted, spent their time, like the American officers in Tizi Ousou, in gambling schools seated on the ship's hatches. On Sunday morning they were cleared from the hatches so that a church service might be held. Only around 20 men turned up and there were only two officers, both of them British, specifically Wilcox and the London Transport official. Wilcox may still have had his religious doubts but as the old saying goes, you rarely find a doubter or an atheist in a fox-hole. Moreover, while they had not been in a land battle, having been in London during the Blitz both Wilcox and the former London Transport man had some idea of what bullets, explosives, shells and shrapnel could do. The G.I.s had no such knowledge or experience, and once the church service ended the gambling schools reassembled.

As the convoy approached the beaches, Wilcox and his two fellow Civil Affairs officers collected their tablets against various forms of sickness, their bug powders, water purifiers and rations. Wilcox was also encumbered with the tools of his new trade: armbands for those that he recruited to positions in local government, proclamations and the stamps and inkpads necessary for, primarily, authorising movements by members of the local population. He also received 200 'Gold Seal Dollars' to meet any necessary expenses.

Thus equipped, on Sunday 12 September, the fourth day of the Allied assault, he climbed aboard a landing craft and headed to the beach. Wilcox may, in fact, have disembarked from the *James W. Marshall* just in time. The German occupation of the Italian airfields ensured that all of the invasion ships were in harm's way; and a number were seriously damaged, including the *James W. Marshall*, which had to be taken in tow back to Britain.

The *Luftwaffe* was also able to strafe the beaches and anyone expecting a welcome by cheering crowds celebrating liberation from a fascist dictatorship was rapidly disabused by a well-organised, ferocious German defence that tore into the Allied troops as they landed.

Wilcox and the two officers with him were met by armoured vehicles and driven to Paestum, which had been at the centre of the U.S. assault and was now relatively secure. Here, however, he and an American officer were instructed to make their way to the command post of the American VI Corps established in a tobacco warehouse about a mile to the north. Most of this part of the journey had to be made on foot, and Wilcox and his companion found themselves having to dive into fox-holes as German fighters sprayed their route with machine gun bullets.

Their uniforms covered with sand, they made their way into a long stone hall hung with tobacco leaves that was buzzing with activity and with messages coming and going over field telephones. They found the Colonel, identified themselves and put themselves at his disposal. The Colonel had a battle to deal with and his response put Wilcox in mind of the Catford station sergeant's reply to the eager Boy Scout who turned up for duty the day war broke out – though no doubt the Colonel's version of 'clear off' was rather more fruity.

Other Civil Affairs officers appear to have faced similar responses. Their proclamations and armbands, even their colt revolvers, were of little value to the ferocious fighting on the beachhead.

Wilcox returned to Paestum where, at the railway station, the Civil Affairs men were beginning to congregate. Military transport, occasionally driven by panicky drivers who on one occasion drove up wearing gas masks in the belief that they had come under gas attack, began to turn Paestum into a depot for petrol, ammunition and general stores. With nothing else to do, the Civil Affairs men sorted out their baggage, washed their clothes, picked figs and peaches to improve their K rations, and sometimes just wandered to gaze at the town's three glorious Greek temples, which dated back to a colony established two-and-a-half millennia before and which were situated about a mile from the railway station.

On the second day in Paestum Wilcox was delighted to see 'Steve' Stephens. He had landed further south on the first day of the landings and, with two American officers, had established himself in Agropoli, a small fishing town with about 5,000 inhabitants. Steve was ready to start his civil affairs duties and had made contact with the Carabinieri lieutenant who was in charge of the district.

Like the French Gendarmerie, on whom they were initially modelled, the Carabinieri were a militarised police. They had played a significant role in the unification of Italy during the nineteenth century and, originally known as the *Carabinieri Reali* (literally the Royal Rifles), they prided themselves on their loyalty to the King. Mussolini had favoured them at the beginning of his rule, but he was always suspicious of this loyalty to the monarchy and developed other police bodies as the Fascist regime had become more entrenched.

As Wilcox and Stephens renewed their acquaintanceship, an Allied Colonel appeared to take command of the idle Civil Affairs men. Wilcox persuaded him that, rather than kicking his heels on the railway station at Paestum, he should be allowed to join the group in Agropoli. He then collected his proclamations and armbands, and set out to liberate the villages to the south of the beachhead.

It was less than ten miles to Agropoli where Stephens and the two Americans had set up a Civil Affairs Office in the town hall. They were, in fact, the first Civil Affairs group to act in Italy under Mark Clark's Fifth Army. The Americans remained at the headquarters in Agropoli while Wilcox and Stephens set off to make contact with the surrounding communes. To facilitate these moves Wilcox procured a jeep with, as the driver, an Italian-speaking American corporal. On the suggestion of Stephens's Carabinieri lieutenant, the first move was another ten miles further south to the lieutenant's own village of Perdifumo. Somehow the locals had news of their arrival and they were met by a large crowd that, somewhat incongruously, greeted them with Fascist salutes; children asked for chocolate and young girls for cigarettes. But Wilcox and Stephens set about the more serious business of formal liberation. Wilcox recalled:

> The local sergeant of Carabinieri led us to the town hall where our Italian-speaking driver informed the mayor and his secretary that they were now under Allied Military Government. Then, accompanied by the mayor and sergeant, now resplendent in the red and black armbands we had given them, we proceeded to the ceremony of posting up the proclamation outside the town hall. Our driver read out the main provisions ordering the villagers to hand in their guns, binoculars and cameras, imposing a curfew after dark and restricting movement without a travel pass. Any breach of these regulations, it was declared, would result in the death penalty. This announcement was greeted with enthusiastic cheers and a forest of Fascist salutes.

It is possible that the Fascist salute was the only demonstration of acclamation that the Italians knew after twenty years of Fascist rule; it is equally possible that the local dialect did not aid understanding, especially when some of the G.I.s who claimed a knowledge of Italian and acted as translators appear often to have had a pretty rudimentary knowledge based on speaking with their more elderly relatives, who were the real immigrants and Italian speakers. Wilcox later commented that the two corporal-drivers that he and Stephens had acquired 'knew much less Italian than they professed.' They were the sons of immigrants, and the accents with which they spoke their limited Italian were 'atrocious.'

As soon as the locals had been advised of details of liberation, Wilcox and Stephens set about the second stage of their task, namely to prepare a report on the state of the territory. They could see what a bad state the local bridges were in and that they would need repair before any heavy rain and resulting fast-flowing rivers in late September. The locals also needed money, decent administration, food, clothing and medical supplies, although once they had assembled the information for their report events began to challenge the extent to which there was indeed a shortage of food, at least among the community leaders. On the insistence of the local priest they had listened to an organ recital in the church and then, while still contemplating how far they might spread the hard biscuits, cheese, chocolate and lemonade powder in their K rations, the Carabinieri lieutenant summoned them to his house for a meal.

> First, the women, not invited to sit with us at the table, brought in plates piled high with macaroni and tomato sauce, followed by dishes of veal and chips. Next came lamb and peppers and then, rather oddly, plates of salami and bunches of grapes. Nor was there any shortage of red and white wine. Somewhat stupefied we settled down to listen to a piano recital by the daughter of the house.

In the late afternoon they returned to their jeep, now festooned with flowers and, amid cheers, clapping and yet more Fascist salutes, they set off to 'liberate' other villages. First they drove due west for about fifteen minutes to Castellabate, and then due west for half an hour to Laureana Cilento. They posted their proclamations and handed out armbands. They had now grown accustomed to the Fascist salutes and responded with V for Victory signs.

At the end of the day they returned to Agropoli and found orders directing them to return to Paestum forthwith. Wilcox and Stephens' liberation sojourn to the south of the beachhead had coincided with a ferocious German counter-attack in which the Americans had suffered heavy casualties and lost ground.

The American commander, General Mark Clark, contemplated several plans for evacuation and reinforcing hard-pressed G.I.s by British troops from elsewhere on the beachhead. Eventually he agreed to fight on; the navy, notably, had pointed to the difficulty of taking beached landing craft back out to sea. Further to the south, the British General Montgomery was ordered to push north from his landing in Reggio Calabria to take pressure off Clark's troops, in spite of the fact that he lacked transport and was hoping to reorganise.

The German counter-attacks lasted for four days, and during this time Wilcox and his comrades could do little more than, once again, twiddle their thumbs on Paestum station awaiting the turn of events. Finally, nine days after the landing on the beaches around Salerno, the Germans broke off the fighting and swivelled to a new defensive line between the Allies and Naples. Wilcox and Stephens and their two American colleagues climbed into their jeeps and drove back to their headquarters in Agropoli.

Like their comrades, and perhaps also like the men who had trained them at Wimbledon, they were novices at their new job. Wilcox rapidly established a pattern for his visits to towns and villages that he was 'liberating.' He explained in a letter to Ethel that he reckoned on driving between 60 to 80 miles each day over rough countryside. On arrival in a town or village he spent possibly as long as two hours interviewing the mayor, his secretary and the chief of police. They seemed to want to argue incessantly among themselves, so Wilcox introduced rules for the meetings: no-one was to speak when he was speaking or his translator was translating, and only one person was to answer a question and to answer it promptly. Occasionally he had to rap on the table, 'look at them fiercely and say I want the answer in one sentence.' At mid-day he and his translator would buy a bottle of wine and eat their rations of biscuits, cheese or bully beef. They usually sat by the side of the road and locals would come and give them grapes, hoping that in exchange they would get cigarettes or, failing that, chocolate.

It occurred to Wilcox and Stephens that their duty was to free the Italians from Fascist rule, yet the people to whom they had given armbands, such as the mayor and his secretary, were invariably people appointed under the Fascist regime. An election might have led to a change of personnel, but they could see no way in which elections could be held in the current circumstances. Potentially there were similar problems with other people of standing in these communities. The Allies had no intention of abolishing the Catholic Church but, wondered Wilcox and Stephens, suppose the local priest had been a collaborator with the regime? Similarly, at least in part the Allies were dependent on the Carabinieri for law and order. The Carabinieri were loyal to the King, but suppose they had felt an equal, even greater loyalty to Mussolini and his authoritarian system? On one of their first visits to a local town, Wilcox and Stephens had taken the advice of the priest and the Carabinieri lieutenant about who should be appointed and who should be replaced. They could not help wondering whether their appointments and replacements had been the right ones. In the event, they satisfied themselves with the fact that there appeared to be general approval of their moves within the communities, even when those moves were made in some haste during tense and difficult situations.

In a letter to Ethel he described having to drive into the hills at the end of September to deal with a rumoured insurrection. The population of a small community had taken the keys of the town hall, refused to obey the local mayor and were resisting handing in their weapons to the Carabinieri because they disliked its local commander. Wilcox called a meeting of leading citizens – the priest, the lawyer, the doctor, a farmer and two shopkeepers – to resolve matters. He dismissed the old mayor, appointed a new one and, through his interpreter, warned that he would have to send in troops if there was any more trouble. The meeting ended with cheers: 'I don't know what they had to cheer about but I've given up trying to understand Italian mentality.' He spent the night in the Carabinieri barracks, where he slept between sheets for the first time since landing and where, in the morning, the Carabinieri brought in the local barber to give him a proper shave.

He then moved on to a second town, as yet not visited by the A.M.G., where the situation was rather more fraught. He described this to Ethel but also, at greater length, in an official report of his experiences written for Sir Frank Brook about a year later. The problem was as much about excessive corruption as local politics.

Again, the crowd had seized the Town Hall:

> On my arrival the Carabinieri Sergeant explained that the people accused the mayor of being corrupt and were dissatisfied with his method of administration. They had locked up the Town Hall and refused to allow any officials to enter but no actual violence had been used. I called a meeting of a representative collection of towns people – the Priest, a doctor, a farmer, a shopkeeper and two labourers – and we decided to appoint a new Mayor. The two candidates in the running were a school-master and a very voluble peasant. The Priest, the doctor and the farmer wanted the school-master, while the others were in favour of the peasant. My casting vote was for the school-master as I had little confidence in the peasant's ability to do anything except make inflammatory speeches.

> When I went out to post up the notice officially appointing the new Mayor I found that the disappointed candidate had been addressing two or three hundred people outside the Town Hall. After warning him that he was disobeying the proclamation by holding a meeting I got my driver to address the crowd, telling them of the appointment of the new man, that he had the support of the Allied Military Government, that the Carabinieri had been instructed to arrest anybody taking part in a meeting or disturbance and that if any trouble did develop armed troops would be sent to the town. To my surprise this announcement was greeted with enthusiastic cheers.

Giving the right people authority and responsibility, with the appropriate armbands, was one concern; using the rubber stamps and ink pads to permit travel or to be out after a curfew was another. Doctors, midwives and other emergency workers were obviously in need of permits, and the issue of such was a constant requirement of Civil Affairs officers as the Allied army slogged up the Italian boot.

But there were occasions when men had to play a situation by ear given the immediate context. Agropoli was a case in point. The principal occupation in the town was catching sardines, and the A.M.G. proclamation prohibited putting out to sea on pain of death. The problem became apparent once Civil Affairs was established in the town. Wilcox and his comrades reckoned that since the Allied navies were active immediately north around Salerno, it would be possible to grant permits for fishermen to work up to 100 yards from the shore. The locals were satisfied and, given the cliental system of the south of Italy which appears to have been abused by the mayor of the town where Wilcox resolved serious disorder, they asked how much they should pay for their permits. The Allied officers refused the offer, apparently to the fishermen's bewilderment.

There were other problems directly related to the aftermath of fighting. There were, for example, regular reports of German soldiers hiding in the vicinity of the communes, and there were other reports of roads being mined. On one occasion, a peasant pointed out what appeared to be a can of petrol; Wilcox, who was then explaining the Civil Affairs job to an American major, picked it up and began to unscrew the top. The American recognised the container as a German mine and yelled a warning; fortunately for Wilcox, it did not explode.

There were also large numbers of disorganised Italian soldiers who wandered along the roads finding their way home; they considered the war, or at least their part in it, to be over. One group lit candles to see their way through a railway tunnel and inadvertently blew up an ammunition train that had been abandoned on their route. And there were other problems that the locals seem to have believed these new administrators could fix. Wilcox remembered a day in the town hall of Agropoli during which, along with the usual requests for travel and curfew permits, he received a deputation requesting that the fixed price of olive oil be raised, a farmer seeking compensation for damage caused when his farm was used as an airfield, and the wife of a P.O.W. in Africa asking that her allowance cheque be cashed. On the same day he was asked to find 50 women from Agropoli who could wash linen at a field hospital in Paestum, together with wicker baskets in which the linen could be carried; he was also requested to round up 1,000 mules to be used by the Fifth Army.

The reports made, and experience gained by Stephens and Wilcox in Agropoli, encouraged the two Colonels in charge of the entire Civil Affairs unit to establish their headquarters there. After their few days visiting the communes around the town, Wilcox and Stephens had become the most experienced officers in the unit and as a result they found themselves sought after for advice and being accompanied on trips around the district by others who were keen to get experience.

It was also an idyllic setting in the late summer. Mountain ranges ran down towards the sea with deep clefts of volcanic rock that contrasted with an ochre-coloured soil, home to cacti and sliver-grey olive trees. Wilcox reminisced that they could have asked for nothing better than the days of driving their hardy little jeeps along twisting roads that overlooked dry riverbeds awaiting the early autumn rains and floods, and continued up to the next white-washed, hill-top village. Idyll and beauty, however, soon gave way to poverty, squalor and violence.

Naples: Squalor, Stench and Swindles

Two weeks after the landing the Allied Military Government set about establishing a more formal organisation for the whole province of Salerno. There were to be five districts, each with an A.M.G. headquarters and staff. For matters of law and order, however, the liberated region was divided into two. P.G. 'Tubby' Green, a Chief Inspector from the City of London Police, was appointed as Public Safety Officer for one half and Wilcox took over the other half, which included the provinces of Naples, Salerno, Avellino and Benevento.

Shortly afterwards the Allies occupied Naples. Wilcox was ordered to the city, where he was appointed chief P.S.O. for the entire Fifth Army and promised a promotion to Lieutenant Colonel, which did not arrive until the following June. His immediate superior in Naples was Colonel Orlando Wilson, an American police officer with a formidable c-v. Most of the American officers in this area of Civil Affairs were lawyers, which meant that the practicalities of dealing with policing problems generally fell to British police officers. Wilson, however, was an exception; and an exception in every way. He had worked as a beat patrolman with the Berkeley Police Department while getting a B.A. with a major in Criminology. His radical ideas about policing had led to trouble with the citizenry where he had first served as Chief of Police. He faced similar problems elsewhere, notably in Wichita, where he fell foul of the racketeers who were deeply entrenched in local government. In 1939 he accepted a tenured position as a full professor at Berkeley, with a limited timetable engineered deliberately to enable him to undertake consultative work on police administration.

Policing and police reorganisation were crucial tasks for the Allies as they occupied Naples at the beginning of October 1943. At the end of November, however, Wilcox was lamenting to Ethel that he was back behind a desk:

> All my life I've been trying to get into some kind of active life, but usually I finish in an administrative position. I thought the police force would be an active job but I've spent most of my life in offices. The first three weeks in Italy were active enough, but now I seem anchored at Regional Headquarters...

Not that Naples was unexciting. He had entered Naples two days after the first Allied troops. The city was in an appalling state. It was under aerial bombardment, and the Germans had left delayed action mines which exploded several days after the Allies had arrived. The electricity system was seriously damaged and, more seriously, so also were the water supply and the sewers. Sea water had to be distilled from the bay. Thousands sought refuge from the bombing in local caves, and the streets and alleys were crowded with the homeless, both native Neapolitans and refugees.

Almost a year after the Allies moved in, the Countess of Ranfurly, secretary to one of the principal British commanders, wrote vividly of the people and their plight:

> The poverty and squalor are heartbreaking. People live in garages and alleys and ghastly houses. The only bright things to be seen are the onions and red vegetables and little birds in cages that hang from the walls. Children, with bare bottoms and no shoes, play in the sickening filth of the streets, building with their own imaginations, castles of manure. Men walk along bent nearly double under the bundles of faggots and vegetables they carry. Donkey carts creak by festooned with scarecrow human beings, their limbs and faces bony with undernourishment. Despite it all the people in these slums seem gay and kind. Here a smiling father leads his grubby child across the cobbled street – there some women sit laughing in a doorway as they

patiently delouse each other's heads.

Norman Lewis, the novelist and travel writer who served as an intelligence officer and arrived in the city at about the same time as Wilcox, painted a similar picture, but without the romantic images of children and smiling parents. He found the city literally collapsing about his ears:

> There was a terrible stench of shattered drains and possibly something worse, and the Middle Ages had returned to display all their deformities, their diseases, and their desperate trickeries... A legless little bundle had been balanced behind a saucer into which a few lire notes and a sweet had been thrown. In a matter of two hundred yards, I was approached three times by child-pimps... We were stopped at a bottleneck caused by a collapsed building ... where a sanitary post had been set up, and here every passer-by was sprayed with a white powder against the typhus.

Disease became rampant, affecting the Allied army but especially the hungry, ill-clad local population. Dysentery and, more seriously, cholera and typhus among the locals, kept the Allied medical staff busy. Yet the principal problem for Wilcox was crime, especially in the form of the black market.

To the British policemen in Civil Affairs, trickery and the black market seemed everywhere in Italy. On 23 December 1943 Wilcox wrote to Ethel about a party that they were organising for children in the area of their headquarters. They had invited around 50 children aged between 4 and 10, but expected many more to turn up and that they would have to turn these away.

Six days later he wrote to her again, rather depressed, after hearing that many of the children had sold the chocolates and sweets that they had been given. 'I suppose they are born racketeers.'

In fact, the shortages under the Fascist regime had already led to a flourishing black market in the south of Italy when the Allies arrived. Arthur Young, formerly the Assistant Chief Constable of Birmingham and now the senior British Public Safety Officer in Italy, often wrote as if the relationship between the Allies and the Italians was akin to a colonial one in which the Italians were, in the understanding of the time, the kind of primitive people that were in need of western Europe civilisation. In his report on the British police serving in Civil Affairs he declared:

> There is no human activity which the Southern Italian cannot transpose into a profiteering swindle. This lack of civic sense is Italy's tragedy. The Italians do not seem to realise that they are cutting each other's throats, or, if they do, they are quite indifferent....

> Typical of this individual short-sightedness is the fact that every day one can see enormous lorries laden with wine travelling to towns where high black-market prices can be obtained, notwithstanding the fact that in these self-same towns, hunger strikes the streets. Food is lacking for want of transport used for the haulage of wine and other non-essential cargos.

What Young ignored here, but what became rapidly clear to every P.S.O. in and around Naples, was the fact that once the docks became the landing point for military supplies, the opportunities for black marketeering mushroomed. This had begun to be a serious problem as soon as the Allies first occupied the port; it was under bombardment particularly from the air and, as Wilcox recalled, there was no time to keep a check on the stores and equipment as they were landed. Things got no better as the bombardment ceased and the Germans moved back.

In April 1944 Norman Lewis recorded the Psychological Warfare Bureau of the Allies, reporting that 65 percent of the *per capita* income of the Neapolitans' income derived from the market in Allied supplies, and that a third of all supplies and equipment landed on the docks disappeared into the black market.

The Allied and the Italian courts became full of small-time receivers and sellers, and the bandits caught in the act of robbery. The organisers and the wealthy gang leaders, if caught and convicted by the local courts, appear generally to have received lesser terms of imprisonment than their foot soldiers. It was also alleged that they lived well in prison. Many of the major offenders were never caught and, while Young and Wilcox were silent on the subject, it appears that some American officers in the A.M.G. provided protection.

Notable among these seems to have been Colonel Charles Poletti, who had close links with a locally-born gangster, Vito Genovese. Genovese had moved to America as a young man and became a gangland enforcer, clawing his way to the top until faced with an indictment for murder. He fled to his native Italy and succeeded in ingratiating himself with the Fascist regime. On the Americans' arrival he switched sides and wormed his way into becoming an indispensable advisor to the A.M.G.; but also had a finger in just about every racket in Naples.

Crime and Police Italian-Style

The British police officers who landed in Italy in 1943 alongside Wilcox had some experience of the wartime black market at home, but this was nothing to match what they found in Italy. The scale of the problem there was far greater than at home, and far more dangerous for those charged with suppressing it. Sicilian mafiosi and the Neapolitan *camorra* were used to carrying weapons and using them.

The boasts of Mussolini that Cesare Mori, his Iron Prefect (*il prefetto di ferro*) in Sicily, had destroyed the mafia in Sicily and that the camorra had virtually ceased to exist were idle. Moreover, there were new bandit gangs made up of armed deserters that took over small towns and villages acting as the new town bosses, and 'protected' their little communities by theft, selling on and by shooting their opponents.

The latter bandit groups were principally the responsibility of the Military Police, whose task it was to deal with military offenders, but Civil Affairs officers could not help but become involved, especially when civilians and deserters were closely mixed, and when it was the Italian Police, some of whom were commanded by Civil Affairs officers, were required to enforce the law.

There were other offences that involved Civil Affairs, as well as the Military Police, and again these were not unknown in Britain, but in Italy they often acquired a new level of ferocity or complexity. Shortly after Wilcox landed at Salerno, several hundred British troops on the bridgehead mutinied over broken promises. This was a British military mutiny and was handled by British authorities, though poorly and, as many thought at the time and subsequently, unjustly. A mutiny by Italian troops, however, came under the remit of Civil Affairs, and Wilcox showed himself an able and effective commander in sorting out one such problem.

In the early hours of 15 February 1944 Wilcox was called on by two Civil Affairs officers, Captain Leslie Tompkins, formerly of the Bedfordshire Police, and Lieutenant J.W. Atkinson, an American from Arlington, Virginia. They explained that they had been requested to supply 250 Carabinieri to deal with a mutiny of an Italian Army Pack Mule Company. The muleteers had been brought out of the line for a rest after nearly two months; but after only a few days they had been ordered back and 250 of them refused to go.

On hearing the account from Tompkins, particularly the fact that an Italian general was planning to have the men disarmed by the Carabinieri, Wilcox was concerned about a pitched battle and good propaganda for the Germans. He made a series of phone calls to ensure that the appropriate senior officers of the Fifth Army were aware of the situation, and received authority to deal with the matter as he thought fit. He then ordered Tompkins to move 250 Carabinieri from Naples to Caserta with one day's rations, but to hold them in reserve and to take no further steps until he received new instructions directly from Wilcox.

Atkinson accompanied Wilcox, who convened a meeting between senior Fifth Army and Italian officers at 7.40 a.m. Tompkins's Carabinieri arrived at Caserta at 11.00 a.m., and 90 minutes later Atkinson accompanied a mixed group of American and Italian officers to where the mutineers were encamped.

By the early afternoon of 16 February, virtually all of the muleteers had agreed to return to the front. Thirty-two were unaccounted for; presumably they had gone absent without leave or deserted. Thirty-eight others were singled out as being the most troublesome and were put in a P.O.W. cage for questioning in order to discover whether there were any subversive elements among them. Wilcox was back in his headquarters by 6.30 p.m. It had taken less than 24 hours to resolve the situation; force had not been used, and no-one had been injured.

At home, British police had experience of servicemen fighting each other in pubs, dance halls and, indeed, any venue big enough and where hostility between units over what were sometimes trivial issues, or inter-service rivalry often aggravated by men coming from different, if Allied, countries. British servicemen were especially jealous of the 'over-paid, over-sexed and over here' American soldiers. It was the same in Italy; soldiers fought each other when on leave or out of the front line, and the situation was worsened by the fact that, until recently, the Italians had been the enemy. In Naples and beyond, different units clashed with Italian soldiers and with Carabinieri sometimes using firearms and grenades as well as the more usual fists, belts and boots of an inter-regimental, inter-service conflict. Wilcox recalled one clash between drunken Canadian soldiers and Carabinieri in Naples which ended with one of the Carabinieri dead and nine others injured. And some of the Allied troops had little or no respect for Italian policemen in general; they thought nothing of disarming a policeman, possibly as a joke, and of releasing any civilian that he had arrested.

Soldiers temporarily away from the front were also troublesome in ways that British policemen had experienced at home, but the trouble appears to have been rather worse when they were conquerors, and it could take on novel twists.

Wilcox reported a pastime adopted among some troops of 'requisitioning' Italian vehicles or other property 'simply by handing the owner a slip of paper usually signed in a facetious manner.'

Soldiers temporarily away from the fighting sought solace in drink and in the arms of women. In Naples particularly, prostitution and the spread of venereal disease among troops were seen as major problems for the Allied armies. There were both professional sex-workers and women desperate enough to sell themselves to the conquerors to provide the necessaries of life for themselves and their families. Italian men were known to attack young women who were noted as going with Allied soldiers; they might also attack the soldier if he was on his own with her. There were rapes by the soldiers. The French colonial troops from North Africa in particular acquired an appalling reputation for violent assaults on Italian women; the number of victims is disputed, but some have put it as high as 60,000, aged between 11 and 86, with 800 men killed trying to defend them or just getting in the way. Wilcox was outraged by the general behaviour of Allied troops in Naples; but many others, especially when assaults on women were concerned, were reluctant to see soldiers prosecuted, and especially when a female victim was known to be a prostitute.

The supervision of prostitutes in established brothels, like many other offences perpetrated by Italian civilians, was left largely to the Italian police. The supervision of these police came under the remit of A.M.G.O.T.'s Civil Affairs section, and for most of his time in the Headquarters of the Allied Military Government this supervision became one of Wilcox's roles. Most of the British police considered the Carabinieri to be the best disciplined and most efficient of the Italian police institutions; and the senior officers of the corps took every opportunity to show their men off in their full-dress uniforms.

Wilcox's sister-in-law, Sophie Marguerite, was stationed briefly in Bari, on the Adriatic coast. She had begun her wartime career as Commandant of an internment camp in Egypt, but early in 1944 she moved to Italy as a member of the Political Warfare Branch. Wilcox contrived to get authority to visit the Carabinieri training in a Replacement Centre in Bari; he intended to assess their readiness to follow the Eighth Army into the Province of Ancona, where they were to co-operate with the army and to re-establish normal policing.

He dressed for Bari as if it was nothing but a working trip, and when he met his sister-in-law for lunch he had driven from the other side of Italy and was still wearing a travel-stained battle-dress blouse and army shorts. It was his intention to drop her off at her office immediately after lunch and then drive to the Carabinieri centre. Unfortunately his jeep broke down; there was no time for any stops when he eventually negotiated a tow.

On arrival at the centre, to his great discomfiture, he found that the Carabinieri commander was intending not merely to discuss matters of equipment, organisation and strength, but wanted to impress his guest – and also his guest's 'wife.' Wilcox told Ethel that when he told the Carabinieri officer that Sophie Marguerite was not his wife 'he gave me a look of complete understanding.'

Stirring music was played in the background by a military band, while mounted and foot Carabinieri were lined up on the parade ground in their best dress uniforms of blue tunics and trousers with red facings, white epaulettes – silver for the officers –, white shoulder belts and their distinctive bicorne, with its ostentatious golden grenade badge and its blue and red feathered plume. Wilcox, almost a foot taller than the Carabinieri commander, had to inspect the parade in his drab, travel-stained khaki and then take a salute as the parade marched out through the entrance gates to display themselves to the people gathered on the sea front. The jeep was repaired; Sophie Marguerite was presented with a bouquet of flowers; and eventually Wilcox was able to leave. 'Our departure', he believed, 'though not impressive had a less ludicrous aspect than our arrival.'

Wilcox suspected that the best of the Carabinieri were, unfortunately, in P.O.W. cages on the other side of the Mediterranean, having been captured during the North African campaign. Other good men were organised into 'legions' of 50 men or more and put under the command of a Civil Affairs officer; it was their task immediately to follow an assault and to establish order in newly occupied territory. Leslie Tompkins, for example, after the mutiny of the muleteers, commanded one such legion from the landing at Anzio, through the occupation of Rome and beyond as the Allies fought their way up the Italian boot.

Yet however loyal to the King, and however proud of their role in the unification and preservation of Italy and the protection of its people, the Carabinieri as a body had never been opposed to the Fascist regime; indeed, some had positively welcomed it. But whether sympathetic to the Allies and putting first their loyalty to the King and his new government established in liberated southern Italy, or secretly lamenting the end of Fascism, members of the corps found themselves in a tough situation once the Allies landed. Wilcox learned quickly that the men around Naples had not been paid for two months and one of his first jobs was to organise their payment in A.M.G.O.T. currency.

Even so, the situation remained bleak for the small squads of Carabinieri in their little barracks in and around Naples. In January 1944 Norman Lewis recorded in his diary how he had entered a Carabinieri station where the *Brigadiere* (essentially the station sergeant/commander) was

> in a state of shock, sitting at his desk staring into space. He was suffering from daily gunfights between rival gangs, bandits, pillaging army deserters, vendettas, kidnappings, mysterious disappearances, reported cases of typhus, the non-arrival of his pay and the shortage of supplies of every kind, including ammunition.

Small wonder, then, that even some Carabinieri became involved in the black market and various other scams. Yet even if some Carabinieri were prey to temptation, Wilcox and others had much less faith in other Italian police institutions.

The Interior Ministry Police had been boosted considerably by the Fascist government and its *Agenti di Pubblica Sicurezza* (Agents of Public Security) were designated as the prime defenders of Mussolini's new order. The *Sicurezza* agents were under the authority of the Ministry of the Interior; they were spread throughout Italy's 96 provinces each of which was administered by a *Questore* (a chief of public security). Whereas the Carabinieri were mainly barracked on the main roads, members of the *Sicurezza* were to be found based in the larger towns where they carried out conventional police patrols and C.I.D. work.

The manner in which they had been fostered and developed by the Fascist regime made them suspect both to the Allies and to many Italians. Wilcox thought also that they had an unenviable reputation for corruption. He wrote to Ethel about an invitation to dine with a

Questore in Naples:

> In spite of all the starving people here we had soup, lobster and mayonnaise, meat and vegetables, pudding coffee, bread, wines and brandy. As he is the chief police official for the province I suppose it all came out of the black market.

The Finance Police (*Guardia di Finanza*) was a military body like the Carabinieri, and among its duties were the patrolling borders and the coastline; as such it was men from the *Finanza* who had been the first to exchange shots with Austrian troops when Italy entered the First World War. Its principal tasks, however, as its name implied, involved enforcing customs and excise, the regulations regarding taxation.

Like the Carabinieri, the *Finanza* were responsible to the Ministry of War, but the Allies decided to move them to the Ministry of Finance in 1944, principally to avoid having to supply them with military rations.

The *Finanza* were the police chiefly responsible for dealing with the black market. Some appeared to have dealt in this market rather than acted against the racketeers, but Wilcox thought them more popular than the Carabinieri and the *Sicurezza*.

Finally there were small numbers of Forest Guards, responsible to the Ministry of Agriculture, and Municipal Watchmen, responsible to their local municipality. These had some police powers, but were mainly tasked respectively with the protection of forests and game and with the enforcement of local by-laws.

In Wilcox's estimation, whether the police contained Fascists or not, the whole police system had been undermined by Mussolini's regime. Many of the British police officers, probably including Wilcox, believed that police officers had to pay at least lip service to the Fascist ideology to keep their jobs during the 1920s and 1930s. Fascism itself had also undermined the police with the creation of its militias with some police powers.

Wilcox also pointed to the destructive effects on policing – and by this he clearly meant an ideal of British policing – that resulted from the appointment of politically compliant senior officers, the use of the police for political oppression most notable in OVRA (*Opera Vigilanza e Repressione dell'Anti-fascismo*), the political police. Equally corrosive was what appeared to be an indifference to corruption, which appeared to have contributed to some police involvement with the black market when the Allies landed.

There was also the use of police, primarily from the *Sicurezza*, for duties such as acting as personal servants to officials. This led Wilcox to predict, gloomily, that 'it will take some time to train them after many years of household chores, shopping and nursemaid duties'; and in retrospect he commented that

> we started off thinking we would reorganise them on English lines. At the end of two years I had come to realise that if you wanted to change the Italian police you would first have to change the Italian people.

The different varieties of Italian police led to overlaps and rivalries between them, while the Allies were confused and frustrated as they sought to make sense of the situation, reorganise it and re-establish a degree of efficiency.

Other police and penal practices from the Fascist years created problems for Civil Affairs in the Italian prisons. There were 74 prisons in the Naples area, but only 40 were available for holding those charged and those convicted; the others had either been too severely damaged in the fighting or were requisitioned as barrack accommodation by the Allies. The problem was aggravated in occupied Naples, as arrests began to average 100 a day and one of the functioning prisons had 700 people awaiting trial. Some of those arrested were imprisoned on the word of an Allied soldier, who then left for the front and was subsequently very difficult to find. Wilcox and his comrades resolved this problem by requiring that every Italian police officer carry arrest slips and report forms that had to be completed by the soldier stating the reasons for the arrest and the man's name, rank and number. The requirement appears to have dissuaded some soldiers from bothering.

Other suspects, however, were held as the result of arrests

by the Italian police, and here the old Fascist practices became apparent. It had been usual to incarcerate a suspect but to proceed with gathering evidence at an extremely leisurely pace. The Allies attempted to speed this up, and rapidly to release those against whom no evidence could be found. It had also been the practice to hold without trial anyone suspected of being a threat to the Fascist state. One enthusiastic *Questore* took it upon himself to continue the practice by arresting and holding without trial former Fascists and those suspected of being a threat to the Allies and the King's new government. Others were arrested on the denunciation of police informers or others, and again, following Fascist practices, no-one bothered to check.

'In some cases', Wilcox recalled '[the police] employed as informers criminals who made considerable fortunes by blackmailing persons whom they threatened to have interned as dangerous Fascists.' He remembered, particularly, the case of a captain in the Carabinieri who was interned for three months for unwitting involvement with such a blackmailer. The captain's superior made no investigation of the case and only after repeated representations to the Public Safety Branch was the captain brought before a court of enquiry made up of Carabinieri officers and two Public Safety officers. No evidence was found against the captain; he was released, reinstated in his rank and posted to a different province. Nothing seems to have been done about his superior who, it appeared, had made a habit of imprisoning any - and everyone - against whom an accusation was made.

In Wilcox's estimation, the Public Safety Headquarters in Naples became rather like an ordinary police station. While they did not wish to become involved in actual operations, they never turned anyone away. They were assisted by three young Italian women secretaries, all of whom were fluent in English. They had been found for them by Freddy Zanchino, a former major in the Carabinieri who had spent much of his life in England and the United States. The women's English was a boon to Wilcox and his comrades, who would otherwise have had to survive on their two Italian lessons at

Tizi Ousou and what they had picked up since their landing. They remained unimpressed with the linguistic abilities of many of the American troops who claimed to know the language.

The problem at the Headquarters, other than the sheer volume of work, was the occasional crackpot who might also be found contacting British police stations. Wilcox explained one such:

> We received a letter from a man who claimed that he had an invention which would shorten the war. This letter had been passed from Headquarters to headquarters until it finally reached Regional Public Safety Division. The inventor turned out to be an eccentric old man of 70 who produced a work of 100 pages describing how, by enclosing an aeroplane propeller in a long metal cylinder, aircraft could fly twice as fast and tanks and motor trucks could ascend vertically from the ground. This treatise was referred to the Professor of Physics at Naples University who confirmed our suspicions that the old man had produced a work of imagination rather than a work of science.

Always the Administrator

As winter turned to spring in 1944, Wilcox found himself posted some 20 miles to the north-east of Naples, to the sumptuous eighteenth-century palace of Caserta. This was the headquarters of General Sir Harold Alexander, the overall commander of Mark Clark's American Fifth Army and Montgomery's Eighth Army. The task at Caserta was to plan the liberation of Rome; in particular to ensure that there was no rioting and looting, that food and shelter were available for the homeless and that deserters and refugees were rounded up.

The staffs of the two armies worked together, but in retrospect Wilcox thought that had the British officers with him been a little more politically minded they would have recognised that the honour of being the first Allies in Rome was destined for Clark's men. This, after all, was going to play very well among the Italian community in New York and elsewhere in the States. Moreover, Clark was surrounded by a battery of public relations people and it was these who probably came up with Clark's story of being the first general to take Rome from the south since the Byzantine Belisarius.

Wilcox set out to correct the Americans' history in his short memoir by stating that the honour ought, in fact, to have gone to the Byzantine Emperor Justinian 200 years later. Everyone seems to have been confused in attempting to score points; Belisarius was Justinian's general. It looked as if the Americans had the wrong date, while Wilcox failed to link the two men.

Arthur Young had met Wilcox on several occasions while visiting his officers in Naples and the surrounding provinces, and Wilcox was not surprised when Young called in on him at Caserta. This was no mere social call. Young had been sufficiently impressed to invite Wilcox to join him at the Allied Commission. Wilcox was reluctant. He had enjoyed being in the field and able to use his discretion without having any superior authority breathing down his neck and telling him what to do. On the other hand, he had been in the army long enough by now to have learned the old dictum: 'Never volunteer; never refuse.' This meant that, once again, he was heading back to the realms of administrative duties; but he believed that, in spite of the promises made earlier it was this move, and Young's support, that brought him his colonelcy.

Colonel Charlie Francis, a veteran of the First World War, a Chief Inspector in the Metropolitan Police and an instructor at Hendon, had taken over as commander of Public Safety in Naples. He decided that, as Wilcox travelled from Caserta to his new office back in Salerno, he should have a bit of a party. As midnight approached on Sunday 19 March the party was in full swing, and Francis's phone rang to inform him that Mount Vesuvius was erupting and that the Fire Brigade was being sent out. Francis thought it some kind of practical joke, and whoever heard of a Fire Brigade extinguishing the eruption of a volcano. He was about to hang up when he glanced out of the window to see a dull red glow and belching smoke across the bay. As for the Fire Brigade, they were attempting to evacuate people from the area and striving to protect the villages close to Vesuvius from the lava flows and flying sparks and cinders.

The Regional Fire and Civil Defence Officer was another British policeman, L.A. Toes, a sergeant from the Scarborough force. He was one of the Civil Affairs officers who had joined Wilcox and Stephens in Agropoli to acclimatise and learn from their experience. It is not clear whether he was at the party, but Young was to single out his role in assessing the situation and the danger to the local inhabitants.

The following morning Wilcox drove from Naples to Salerno. Vesuvius was still showering cinders the size of walnuts, while the locals held umbrellas to protect themselves as they trudged through dust and cinders inches deep. The depressing grey of these cinders and dust was an omen for the bureaucratic procedures in which Wilcox soon found himself enmeshed. It was a daily grind of reading, taking minutes and preparing reports, attending meetings and drafting directives, all quite different from the relatively carefree improvisation that he had enjoyed in liberated towns and then in supervising, but still engaged in the procedure with a light touch over his men.

The situation was complicated by the fact that Young did not get on with the American Colonel with whom he was deputed to work in the sub-commission for public safety. Initially, the Allies in Italy liked to have an American working alongside a Briton. Colonel Kirk was technically the superior in the relationship but he was a lawyer, while Young was a policeman. They appear to have both had strong personalities, but they viewed the task from the perspective of their different backgrounds. The British view was that in Public Safety departments the American lawyer was to be found at the front of the office, chewing on a cigar with his feet on the desk alongside an empty in-tray and an empty out-tray. Behind him was a British policeman, his feet down, his shoulders hunched, writing furiously as he worked through a high in-tray and filled the out-tray. Wilcox was one of the men who worked at the back, taking Young's place as he avoided the office, and Colonel Kirk, to make trips around Italy and to the islands of Sicily and Sardinia.

In his report prepared for Sir Frank Brook in October 1944, Wilcox provided a rather more restrained and thoughtful analysis of the difference between British and American Public Safety Officers. He divided the Americans into three categories. The first of these were the regular police officers who were simply not suitable for administrative work in a foreign country. There were one or two exceptions to this rule, and he singled out Lt. Col. O.W. Wilson here. His second category contained police officials who were mainly political appointees at home and who had little idea of police duties. The third category, which included lawyers and other professional men, had no police experience whatsoever, and had simply been assigned to Public Safety. Even from among this group, Wilcox complained, it was almost impossible to get a written report.

Gradually, he explained, the Americans appeared to drift out of Public Safety, and he noted, perhaps with some satisfaction, that of the 13 Regional Public Safety commanders at the date of his report, no less than 12 were British; while of a total of 141 officers performing Public Safety duties, 104 were British and only 37 American. The problem was that the Allied governments still wanted the interleaving of officers in Civil Affairs, and incompetent as Wilcox and Young thought their American colleagues to be, they kept on coming. 'I am trying very hard not to be too pro-British (i.e. anti-American)' he wrote to Ethel in December 1944,

> but I am afraid my patience is gradually becoming exhausted. I've always considered myself to be very long-suffering but it is only the thought of trying to preserve Anglo-American amity which constrains me to carry on until the New Year before speaking my mind and clearing out from HQ.

In the New Year Arthur Young had accepted the post of Chief Constable of Hertfordshire, leaving a 'hopelessly incompetent' American as head of the P.S.B. Branch of the Allied Government. Everyone appeared to agree the man's unsuitability for the job, and telegrams to this effect were sent to Washington.

As well as working with the Americans, Wilcox's duties involved regular contact with members of the Italian government established in liberated areas of the south now referred to as the King's Italy. The Allied Commission insisted that it be consulted on the appointment of ministers and senior officials such as police commanders, fire officers, prison governors and public prosecutors. At times this, and the contrast between Allied Military Law which was imposed after the landings and its gradual replacement by Italian Law, could lead to difficulties. 'In the jail at Salerno,' recalled Wilcox,

> an Italian was lying under sentence of death passed by a military court. Before execution could be carried out Salerno became part of King's Italy. No death penalty was provided by Italian law and the minister informed the Allied Authorities that he had no power to carry out the sentence. Nor, it appeared, had the Allied Commission or the Commander in Chief. For some time it seemed that this impasse must leave the wretched prisoner in limbo; but finally it was resolved, harshly it may be thought, that military authority must not be flouted and the Cheshire Regiment was ordered to turn out a firing squad.

In southern Italy two ways had been found to relieve the grimness and grind of the job. The countryside around Naples was beautiful and, when the opportunity arose, jeeps were borrowed to drive the delightful corniche around to Amalfi or to other towns, and to gaze out over the sea to the Isle of Capri. On his travels Young found a luxurious, but deserted villa in the coastal town of Positano. He requisitioned it for the use of Public Safety officers, who were able to sit on the flat roof of its tower and gaze out over the sea. There was also a small beach, visited by a few fishermen, which provided Wilcox and his comrades with the opportunity for swimming. The war seemed far away, and so too did mind-numbing, but essential bureaucracy, when these opportunities could be enjoyed. But the pleasures of the corniche and the villa were quickly lost when orders came for the whole Commission to move to Rome.

Rome had been declared an Open City after the cessation of Allied bombing in August 1943. The status held and on 4-5 June 1944 Mark Clark's Fifth Army marched in unopposed. It seemed to Wilcox that most of the planning to restore and maintain public order, with which he had been involved at Caserta, had been unnecessary. This is not to deny that many of the problems of the black market, the theft of Allied materiel, prostitution, drunkenness and violence were similar.

At the beginning of 1945 Wilcox authorised an issue of automatic weapons to Carabinieri in Rome to deal with a gang of bandits led by an 18-year-old hunchback and based in the catacombs after they had shot a British Military Policemen.

It was rather more that the scale of banditry and violence in Rome does not appear to have been quite as dangerous and difficult as that in Naples. The anticipated looting and floods of ragged, sick, half-starved refugees for which the Allies had planned did not materialise. The concerns that Wilcox had personally for the treasures of the Vatican also proved to be unfounded; three British Public Safety officers, including Leslie Tompkins with his Carabinieri legion now bloodied from the beach at Anzio, successfully ensured the protection of the Holy See.

In the wake of the Allied entry into Rome the Allied Commission decided that it should move from Salerno to the established capital of Italy. Wilcox himself used the opportunity of the move to arrange his own jaunt from the west coast across to the Adriatic; if Young could move around the Italian boot freely, why should his deputy not take the opportunity to do something similar?

In Rome, it was back to the grind of Allied Commission bureaucracy, working from 8.30 in the morning to 5.30 in the evening, sometimes even later, in a modern office block built by Mussolini in the Piazza Barberini.

Shortly after they had begun their civil affairs tasks Wilcox and 'Steve' Stephens had wondered together about how many of those they were issuing with arm-bands as Allied representatives had once had Fascist links. It was noted earlier how many British police officers thought that former Fascist police officers were 'Fascist' because they were expected to be. Now Wilcox and some of his comrades began to wonder if the Allied Commission was the right place to be deciding who should, and who should not, be given responsibilities because of their role under Fascism. The policy seemed to be depriving the country of some its more able administrators and business men, and he did not consider that the *scheda personale* that was required to be completed by anyone who was called upon to account for their activities provided the Allies with sufficient evidence to make the necessary decisions.

Wilcox's personal area of authority, the police, faced the problem of people settling old scores by denouncing their neighbours; in one spectacular incident a former Fascist was lynched by a Roman crowd on his way to trial. He was concerned about scapegoats being selected such as the commander of the Carabinieri, a 'poor old boy [who] was doing his best' but who was dismissed 'by a panic stricken government.' He worried about the Allies using torture to extract confessions from suspected spies, and argued with a comrade who had been involved. Hundreds of innocent men and women were denounced and had to be investigated and then were usually cleared from the prisons.

At the same time, the advancing armies had to be relieved as quickly as possible from the need to suppress any civil disorder; this meant bringing effective Italian police into newly liberated areas. Wilcox began to get annoyed with the Romans who, he believed considered that their liberation meant that the war was over, and now they wanted petrol, cars and food; they ignored their poverty-stricken neighbours and were growing increasingly good at criticising the Allies.

'In the country and even in Naples and Salerno,' he told Ethel, 'I had a certain amount of sympathy with [the] people... Here I have lost all sympathy - with the officials at any rate and I am not disguising my feelings.'

The situation was increasingly complicated across the country by the demands of partisans who had fought the Fascists and the Germans. They were suspicious of the Italian police, who they saw as little better than their Fascist predecessors; and after all they were often the same men. Many of the most effective fighting units among the partisans were Communists, which made them automatically suspicious of the Americans and the British, as well as hostile to the Italian King and his government.

Perhaps the partisans were right in their suspicions of the King's government. In his report to Brook, Wilcox expressed little faith in what he considered to be ministers whose main concern appeared to be their own future, and permanent officials who seemed to him for the most part to be incompetent, venal and lacking in initiative and resolution. 'Their general attitude is to wait for the Allies to suggest to them what should be done and then to find excuses for not doing it, or at any rate for postponing action.' There were exceptions, and he gave the example of the Italian Director General of Public Security who had expressed concern to the Prime Minister about political parties illegally collecting arms and ammunition. The problem here was that the government was a coalition of different groups, including some of those who were arming. The Prime Minister attempted some persuasion, which was ignored. Action was only taken when the Allies had insisted that the law be enforced.

The pressure of work in Rome was greater than he had in Naples, and there was no Positano with its glorious countryside, sea views and small bathing beach. Wilcox's hotel on the Via Veneto was a five minute stroll from his office in Piazza Barberini; but there were few opportunities for rest and relaxation and little time to enjoy them. Early in the morning he borrowed a horse from the Carabinieri and went for a ride in the nearby Pincio Gardens; he was always accompanied by an Italian police officer who rode half-a-dozen paces behind him. At the end of the working day, when it was reasonably cool, he did his best to explore the city, usually in company with one of his comrades. He confessed to being a little disappointed that so much of Rome's Classical and Renaissance splendour had been lost, but he still found things to hold his interest. Evenings were spent in the Officers' Club overlooking the Flaminium Way, and again easy walking distance to his hotel. It was, however, always preferable to wangle an invitation to the French Officers' mess as a guest; presumably the cuisine was rather more elegant. Italians often held parties and receptions, but Wilcox was often too tired to take much interest. Occasionally there was a sporting fixture. At Christmas 1944 Wilcox played centre half in a football match that pitted officers against other ranks.

Yet all in all, while it may have been bureaucratic drudgery, his role was not a dangerous one for a soldier and, given that he was now a

Lieutenant Colonel, he was never going to get the excitement that he had known in the days following the landing in Salerno when he was a novice in Civil Affairs. Many of the men who were his juniors were now engaged in the dangerous role of what the Army termed Spearhead Officers, a significant development since the early days. It was their task, usually with a unit of up to about 50 Carabinieri, to move hot on the heels of an assault to begin a rapid clear up and the restoration of order and services. Unfortunately, in the smoke and confusion of battle some Spearheads became spear-points and facing German troops rather than just clearing up after a successful attack. On one occasion this happened to Leslie Tompkins, though he and his Carabinieri were able to extract themselves before having to engage with the enemy. Another Spearhead, an inspector from the Metropolitan Police, was less fortunate in the assault on Florence and was seriously wounded when his Carabinieri unit found themselves in the front line facing German troops.

It was not that Wilcox longed for the sound, fury and danger of battle, but rather that he wanted something more interesting than the dull thud of typewriter keys, negotiating with foreign ministers and civil servants, reading and writing interminable reports, constantly having to take over command of the whole P.S.O. Branch, and then to be replaced by someone he considered to be incompetent. In October he told Ethel that he was rapidly losing interest in Italy, partly because of the way he felt that he was being treated. Arthur Young, he wrote, had already lost interest and was planning on moving back to England, and that was where Wilcox saw his opportunities. Young and Sir Frank Brook would support him. 'What I am really after is the Chief Constableship of a county.' He was embarrassed over thinking about himself in the middle of a war. 'All I really want is to come back and provide you with a reasonably comfortable home and to give Susan and Bridget ... a happy time.'

Nothing materialised over the Christmas period, apart from Young's departure for Herts, and Wilcox finding himself passed over again for permanence in the more significant role that he was repeatedly taking in the Public Safety Branch. The British replacement for

Young was an Assistant Chief Constable from Scotland who was well over 50 years old, and at the leaving party for Young made a speech naming an American officer as the man leaving.

At the end of January 1945 Wilcox came up with a plan for getting back to England. He persuaded the Italian Government that it should send a police mission to study the British system. Alongside the Director of the Scientific Police School in Rome, a representative from the Ministry of the Interior and his helpful Carabinieri friend Freddy Zanchino, he proposed himself as the most suitable man to accompany the group. Young backed the idea, but the discussions in London seemed to go on and on. Then he heard that the War Office wanted experienced police officers in north-west Europe. Young encouraged him to volunteer, and Wilcox found himself appointed to the Military Government for Austria, which was then being formed. It would not get him home immediately, but at least it would give him a change of scenery.

Yet the move to Austria was not quite the end of his involvement with Italy. In August 1945 it was proposed that the Allies should establish a police mission that would travel to Italy assist in reorganising the Italian police system. Wilcox was asked for advice, and he prepared a long paper on the police and an 'unofficial' report for G.H.G. Anderson, who was involved with discussions in the Home Office. The paper was blunt, and showed Wilcox to be full of the prejudices about national characteristics that were common at the time:

> Even before the Fascist regime the Italian Police Service never reached a high standard. This may largely be caused by defects in the Italian character, but the service itself is constitutionally unsound, consisting as it does of five separate forces with considerable confusion and overlapping of responsibility.

Anderson responded with a letter of gratitude. Without Wilcox's comments he felt he would have been 'in a complete fog: as it was I found myself better informed than any of the experts!' Yet as is often feared to be the result of such top level meetings, the discussion largely focussed around two rather pointless matters: '(a) who is to be head of the Commission? and (b) what clothes are they to wear?' In the event neither mattered, since the Italian coalition government would not agree to any such mission; some objected to the Allies telling them that their institutions were inadequate and poorly managed. The British, however, believed that the Communists in the coalition, possibly with Soviet prompting, were the main cause of the refusal.

CHAPTER 5

AUSTRIA

Almost a Summer Holiday

John R.H. Nott-Bower, one of the four Assistant Commissioners of the Metropolitan Police, had been appointed Inspector General of the British Public Safety Branch for Austria in the late summer of 1944. His father had been Commissioner of the City of London Police and he had begun his career in the Indian Police Service, where he was decorated for bravery following the arrest of a group of bandits, during which he had been wounded in the arm. He had not seen any Civil Affairs service during the war, and while he had the reputation for being a competent administrator, he appears to have been among those who saw no reason to change anything in the British Police and, at least by the end of the 1940s, was noted for appearing to take rather more interest in bridge and riding.

Towards the end of 1946 he published the official account *Public Safety in Austria*, which chronicles the story over the two years following the creation of his headquarters in Italy in August 1944. He makes hardly any reference to Wilcox in this account, though much of the description of events in Vienna appears to be drawn, sometimes word for word, from a closely typed, 21-page report signed by Wilcox and now among his family's papers. Perhaps if the senior officers in the two other Austrian provinces that made up the British Zone of the country had left similar papers with their family, it may have been seen that Nott-Bower's account was generally a cut-and-paste job.

The first British Public Safety Officers entered Austria from Italy on 8 May 1945. A small party, escorted by Military Police jeeps, established themselves in the small town of Villach, notable - or perhaps notorious - for its *Bürgermeister* Oska Kraus, who had been a staunch Nazi and who bore the same name as a prestigious Czech philosopher and jurist who had converted from Judaism to Protestantism and escaped to Britain during the war. On the same day Wilcox received orders to travel to Udine, where he was to await instructions on travelling to Austria.

Wilcox was authorised to use a staff car for his journey to Udine. He was also given two fellow officers as travelling companions: George Brooke, from the Bradford City Police, and Edward 'Teddy' Croft-Murray, Assistant Keeper of Prints and Drawings in the British Museum, who was serving as a 'monuments man' or, more formally, a member of the Allies' Monuments, Fine Arts and Archives Sub-Commission, whose duties involved the protection and preservation of art treasures in war-zones.

Croft-Murray was keen to see some of the cultural heritage of Italy; his travelling companions needed little persuading. For one thing, he appeared to be the ideal travel companion-cum-guide. Moreover, the three of them reasoned that rushing to Udine would only mean spending longer in a transit camp awaiting their next set of travel orders. On their first afternoon after leaving Rome, they stopped to wander round Assisi. As the sun set, the three of them gazed out over the Umbrian plain and drank wine. In the quiet surroundings they listened to the radio to hear speeches by George VI and Winston Churchill on the German surrender while London noisily celebrated V.E. Day. The next day took them to Perugia, and from there they moved on to Padua. Next came Venice, though they had little desire to stay long here, since the city was teeming with boisterous Allied troops speeding around in jeeps or travelling up and down the canals in various motorised craft. A surviving photograph shows that Wilcox found some sort of traditional boat with an oarsman and made a canal trip, before the trio climbed back into their staff car and proceeded to Udine.

Udine and its environs were also swarming with troops. The Allied soldiers were exuberant, looking forward to demobilisation and to going home now that the war was over. Alongside them, however, were dejected men in field grey. Most were no less happy about the end of the war than the men in khaki, but they had lost and were now headed for internment camps. Wilcox could not help but feeling some sympathy for the miserable veterans of the other side.

His stay in Udine, however, was brief. There was just enough time to attend a church service giving thanks for victory before he was ordered across the border to Klagenfurt, the principal city of the province of Carinthia, which, with the neighbouring province of Styria, was to form the British Zone of occupied Austria. Klagenfurt became the headquarters town of the British Eighth Army, reconstituted in July 1945 as British Troops in Austria (BTA), and here Wilcox found the British Military Government destined to take control of the British Zone of Vienna. The Military Government was stuck, as the Red Army, which had captured Vienna, was being very slow in letting its western Allies to join it in the city. However, the Public Safety Officers destined for Vienna were welcomed by their counterparts in Klagenfurt for the temporary assistance that they were able to provide.

Wilcox himself drafted instructions regarding the possession of firearms by farmers and hunters; and he drafted advice on the wearing of political armbands and badges. These 'political favours' worried him, given that they were intended to influence people. 'It is a very short step from "influencing" citizens to intimidating them.' From here he took a very long step, probably excessive, but in the context of his experiences over the previous ten years, explicable:

> Our previous experience of the Fascist party in England should serve as a warning. The wearing of Black Shirts led to organised hooliganism and eventually ended in street fights with the Communists. When the Home Secretary banned the wearing of Black Shirt uniforms the Fascist Party became innocuous.

The wearing of political party uniforms is a Nazi and Fascist system, closely allied to militarism, which ought to be suppressed at the outset.

◆

The war may have been over, but there were considerable problems in its aftermath. Around Klagenfurt these problems came principally in two forms: refugees and Yugoslav partisans. Thousands of 'displaced persons' (D.P.s) wandered through the area; some were trying to get home after having been conscripted for labour in, or imprisoned by, the Third Reich; others were fleeing from the Soviets or else from the reconstituted, and expanding Yugoslavia.

At the same time, Yugoslav partisans – generally referred to as 'Jugs' by the British – thronged the area seeking to extend their territory at gun-point. Many Austrians were scared of them; British officers, often alone or with very little back-up, courageously confronted them and generally forced them to back down. Some people feared that there would be fighting. Wilcox wrote to Ethel that they had orders to carry their arms with them, but he also thought that if the British showed enough determination, the 'Jugs' would go quietly. He turned out to be right and the situation was never as bad as in the disputed territory around Trieste.

Yet even with the problems, Wilcox found the summer of 1945 in Carinthia to be enjoyable. He found excellent accommodation with a baroness who kept a riding stable with four good horses. She reminded him of Miss Rogman through whom he had met Ethel; though she was 'a rather more horsey type.' There was swimming in the Wörthersee, once a summer resort for the Viennese nobility; it was possible to find horses for riding in the region; and evenings could be spent drinking the local wine and watching the nearby mountains turn ochre as the sun set.

Another friend from Hendon, Frank Massingberd-Munday, had brought his fishing rods. Massingberd-Munday was soon after to distinguish himself by pretending to be a renegade British officer in a successful undercover operation which unearthed a significant arms dump of S.S. men and broke up an escape route which they had established. But, for the moment, he enjoyed his fishing in the local rivers and occasionally Wilcox accompanied him.

Massingberd-Munday had found an abandoned Fiat and he cheerfully handed this over to Wilcox when he learned that he was dependent on Army transport and had none of his own. Initially the Fiat needed some work to get it into decent running order, but Wilcox was delighted when the military authorities agreed to accept the car as his official transport. The Army agreed to maintain it and supply petrol, and it served him well until shortly before the end of his service when he lent it to his deputy, John 'Jock' Reid, a former Bradford City Police inspector. Reid left it outside his billet for an hour, during which time the car disappeared. 'There is no prospect of getting it back,' Wilcox told Ethel. 'It was almost certainly driven out of Vienna at once and is probably somewhere in Lower Austria or possibly on its way to Russia.'

After he had been in Carinthia for a month during the early summer of 1945 Wilcox and the Vienna contingent were informed that an agreement with the Soviets for their move to the city was near. But in the style to which he had become accustomed, the move was not to be directly from Klagenfurt; rather it was necessary to return to Udine and await the outcome of further discussions between the four powers. Udine was still swarming with troops, and Wilcox and his party were ordered to Maniago, a small town about 30 miles to the west.

Stories filtered through to them about mass rapes and looting by the Red Army in Vienna; and on a much lighter note they were surprised by stories that the Soviets had replaced the Viennese traffic police with women from the Red Army – stories that were not untrue. They began to learn a few words of German and discussed what they hoped to do in their posting to Vienna. It hit Wilcox how little he knew about the Austrian police and particularly those in Vienna; he vaguely remembered a paper in the first edition of the *Metropolitan Police College Journal* written by one of his fellow students at Hendon, Edward Millett Wood, who had left the police in

1940 and volunteered for Army service.

Wilcox decided to use his 'new' Fiat to visit old comrades and subordinates still acting as Civil Affairs officers in northern Italy. He also drove across to Trieste were he found three old friends: Frank Armstrong of the Northumberland Police, with whom he had served in Italy, and two Metropolitan Police officers, Gerry Richardson and Andrew Way, who had graduated from Hendon and were still serving in Civil Affairs in Italy. All three were involved in trying to sort out the problems of the Trieste region where Italians and Slavs confronted each other.

In Maniago, as in Klagenfurt, however, it was easy to be distracted by the opportunities for hill walking, horse riding and swimming. At the same time Wilcox, like thousands of others, continued to think about his future career and also the fact that he had not been home for two years; nor, during that period, had he seen his wife and two young daughters, the youngest of whom was only recently born when he had left for war.

Recognising that some of the senior police officers who had remained in post during the war were now ready for retirement, Wilcox looked for a senior appointment at home. At the very least, he thought, he could get an invitation to an interview which would mean a trip to England. Arthur Young had been appointed as Chief Constable of Hertfordshire; Eric St. Johnston had moved from Oxfordshire to Durham; and Herman ('Graham') Rutherford, on the same course as Wilcox at Hendon, who had shared the expensive European holiday in Duveen's fast car, and who had served alongside him in Italy, had got the Oxfordshire post.

Wilcox was invited for interview in West Suffolk and the City of Liverpool. The only way home was to take a flight from Naples, and he decided to make the long drive from Maniago to Naples in his recently-acquired Fiat. On modern roads the journey of over 500 miles takes around ten hours; on the war-torn roads of Italy it was a hard, rough, bouncing trip, but his car served him well and he was able to visit Public Safety Officers as he drove down the boot. In Naples he made contact with his former interpreters who he now considered friends; and then it was the aircraft for England.

Wilcox failed to secure either of the posts for which he was interviewed. He always believed that he gave a poor performance in interviews, and that he responded to questions with uninteresting, monosyllabic answers. He was pleased that the West Suffolk post went to the deputy Chief Constable there, while the Liverpool post went to the man that he had replaced at Gerald Road in the Metropolitan Chelsea Division.

But the trip was most pleasing since, before flying from Croydon back to Naples, he could spend a few days with Ethel and his daughters. For most of the period since he had left for Italy they had been living on the farm belonging to Ethel's father in the Mendips. The fact that the farm was rather primitive, with neither electricity nor running water, seemed as nothing to Ethel. Her father had moved back to Bristol; she had a girl, an evacuee from London, who helped her, and she was able to visit her family and old friends in Bristol. Wilcox was relieved that she was there when German 'V' weapons began to hit London in the summer of 1944. If only for a short time, the interviews gave him a short period with the family that he had left over two years before, and who he had only seen growing up through the small photographs that Ethel had sent regularly.

On his return to Naples, Wilcox learned that the British Military Government team had at last been given permission to move to Vienna. He retrieved his Fiat from the Neapolitan garage where he had parked it, made the long hard journey back to Udine and from there back into Carinthia. At Bruck, about 100 miles north-west of Klagenfurt, he checked on to the military corridor that ran through the Soviet Zone for just under another hundred miles to Vienna.

Vienna: Four Elephants Aboard a Skiff

Flying from airfields in Italy, American and British bombers had begun hitting targets in and around Vienna in March 1944, and there was a ferocious air bombardment a year later. In January 1945 Hitler designated Vienna to be a *Festung*, a fortress that was to be defended to the end. The Viennese had little interest in the idea, especially as the Allied bombing intensified and the Red Army pressed closer and closer. By the end of March, Nazi authority in the city was noticeably crumbling. The *Gauleiter* Baldur von Schirach declared martial law on 30 March. Six days later he left the city; the Soviets were on the outskirts. The Viennese began looting shops for whatever they needed or thought they might find useful to barter. They slaughtered livestock and emptied wine cellars both to eat and drink heartily, and to prevent the Red Army from enjoying the meat and drink. Vienna fell on 13 April after relatively little resistance.

When Wilcox arrived at the end of the summer, rubble from Soviet artillery fire and from the closer fighting still littered the streets. Many Viennese were nervous about leaving their homes in case Red soldiers should loot what little remained of their possessions. Wilcox could not help but notice cheerful, smiling Soviet troops showing off with two or three watches on their wrists.

It had been decided to divide Austria, like Germany, into four zones: one American, one British, one French and one Soviet. In the summer of 1945 this appeared to be working tolerably well. Vienna, like Berlin, had also fallen to the Red Army and was in the Soviet Zone; and again like Berlin, it was decided that it be divided between the Allied powers. The central *Bezirk* (district) of the city was designated as an international area. The remaining 22 *Bezirke* were divided into clusters among the four powers. The British had responsibility for five of these in the south of the city (*Bezirke* 3, 5, 11, 12 and 13).

On the plus side, their zone included the magnificent 1,400-room baroque Schönbrunn Palace, which the British delegation of the Allied Occupation requisitioned and where the British Army of Occupation established its headquarters; Wilcox's own headquarters was about four miles due east on Reisnerstrasse. There was, however, a major minus to the British position. While the French were to the north, there were Soviet *Bezirke* to the east, and two others (*Bezirke* 4 and 10) split the British Zone in two; equally difficult, to the west and the south was the Soviet Zone of Austria. Moreover, the Soviets appeared reluctant to leave the British Zone and for some time they continued to occupy some buildings and billets. The complex division of the city, Wilcox recalled an Austrian politician saying, was like having four elephants aboard a skiff.

The Public Safety Officers of the four powers came to the table with different aims and expectations. Wilcox had nine officers serving under him; each one was a professional police officer from either an English or a Scottish force. The senior American P.S.O. was a fireman, though one of his deputies, Norman Kinley, was a police officer from Minneapolis; none of Kinley's subordinates were police professionals. Moreover, while Wilcox and his immediate superiors were keen to reorganise the Viennese police, the Americans were more concerned with military police issues. The French Commandant Amstoutz had de-Nazification at the top of his agenda and wanted everyone in Vienna to complete a *Fragebogen* explaining what they had done under the Nazi regime. It took time for the Public Safety Officers of the western Allies to make contact with each other, but it was even more difficult to find their Soviet counterpart. Eventually Major-General Nikolai Travnikov, a celebrated commander of Airborne troops, appeared as the Soviet representative. Given his superior rank, he was appointed to chair a preliminary meeting, held on 8 September, to discuss the future of the Viennese police. There were five men present: one each from the Americans, the British and the Soviets, and two French officers. Travnikov appeared surprised by the suggestion that the reorganisation of the Viennese police should be a matter for a committee of Public Safety. He was never seen again and a Colonel, with a commissar at his shoulder, appeared at future meetings, though reluctant to agree to anything before informing Moscow.

On 17 September the inaugural meeting of what became known as the Public Safety Committee was held; it comprised officers from each of the four powers and the senior officers of the Vienna police. The meeting decided that its chair would rotate, with the position being held by an officer of the same nationality as the presiding general; a post that also rotated among the four powers. There were weekly meetings until the following March, when it was agreed to change the name to the Public Safety Temporary Committee and it only met then when the general presiding over the city considered it necessary. Wilcox wrote gloomily to Ethel that the name change would mean nothing:

> Everybody will drift in except the Russian. We shall give him ten minutes grace and then start. Eventually he will arrive and then the Chairman will have to get an interpreter for him as it would never occur to him to bring his own. Then he will have to have the minutes of the previous meeting read to him as he will say that he didn't receive his copy during the week. All this will take half an hour.

But Wilcox was quite wrong about the inaugural meeting of the Temporary Committee. 'The Russian didn't turn up at all.' He wondered whether he had been frightened by Wilcox having put a motion regarding inter-Zone arrests on the agenda. 'I was looking forward to a little plain speaking' about Soviet behaviour in the British Zone and he was not going to avoid the matter, inserting it once again on the agenda for the next meeting.

In addition to his continuing arguments with the Soviets, Wilcox also prepared monthly reports with sections on crime, the police, the behaviour of Allied soldiers, and the more successful debates between the Allies. A large number of issues were relatively easily and amicably resolved, such as the problem of synchronising time – the western Allies, the Viennese and the Soviets were all working to different times.

Equally, there were few difficulties in issuing troops with garrison passes, written in the four languages of the occupiers and differently coloured for the men of different armies: white for the Americans, green for the British, blue for the French and red for the Soviets. The aim of theses passes was to control troops wandering the streets without authority and often committing offences; a general lack of military discipline appeared to be the greatest problem in the city. Similarly, although the Soviets were keen to restrict the movement of civilians, it was agreed to raise the curfew, particularly to enable the Viennese to undertake work on essential services such as gas and electricity after dark, or making bread, a task that was commonly undertaken at night. Unfortunately, the existence of the passes and the end of the curfew for Viennese citizens appeared to have had little impact on the behaviour of many Red Army soldiers; similarly, more senior Soviet personnel appeared to think that they could deal with the locals with impunity.

Wilcox's difficult diplomatic issues with the Soviets were largely the result of the way in which the British Zone was surrounded and divided by Soviet *Bezirke*, and the way in which some of the Soviet Allies that had missions in Vienna tended to copy Soviet behaviour. The Yugoslav Mission had two agencies in the British Zone, and these were noted for employing high-handed behaviour and brutality. Early in 1946 Viennese police, backed by British patrols, carried out a raid on the Veterinary High School in *Bezirk* 3. They arrested two Yugoslavs, members of a gang that had been engaged in trafficking on the black market; a considerable quantity of property, including food-stuffs, tools and vehicle parts, were found in their possession. The two men were handed over to the Yugoslav Mission and sent home. The Mission itself did not appear to have black market involvement, and denied all knowledge of the property, but shortly afterwards it began claiming that the police return property. The British demanded proof of ownership, and the Yugoslav demands were promptly changed to the effect that the Viennese police should provide a list of the property seized. On British instructions these demands were also refused.

The Soviets could behave similarly, as when an Austrian and two Czechs were arrested for black market offences in *Bezirk* 5. The day following the arrests a woman claiming to be the secretary of an officer in the Central Soviet Kommandatura turned up at the district police station and demanded their release on the grounds that they were Soviet citizens. Captain Thomas Greenhill, formerly a detective sergeant in the Metropolitan Police, was the P.S.O. in command of the district and he refused the demand. The three prisoners were moved to the Central Prison, which was situated in the American Zone, and two days later the same woman turned up and successfully demanded that they be released. Unlike the Yugoslavs, she also managed to get the property seized in the affair: 24,474 cigarettes and 30,000 Allied Government *Schillings*. Perhaps she was not the secretary of a Soviet officer, but just a very cool criminal operator. Either way, other Soviet activities had a similar ring.

On 19 October 1945 the four commanding generals in Vienna agreed to the Allied Inter-Zone Arrest Agreement. This prohibited any member of one of the Allied occupying powers from taking it upon himself to enter the zone of another power to arrest an individual suspected of a crime or of being a threat to security. Henceforth, any such entry and arrest required the knowledge and consent of the occupiers of the zone where the suspect was believed to be.

Four months later Major Witt, the commander of the Red Army's Military Police in Vienna, called at the British Public Safety Headquarters and asked for authority to arrest deserters in the British Zone. His request was refused on the grounds that when, a few weeks earlier, he had received such permission, his men had arrested a number of civilians, including a number of Poles. Witt continued to be denied authority, even when he insisted that he had received such permission from the Americans. Subsequently it was found that this was untrue; and it was also found that he had called on the French, equally unsuccessfully, telling them that both the Americans and the British had granted such permission.

Franz Sverak, a railway employee who lived in *Bezirk* 17 in the American Zone, informed a Soviet officer that he had witnessed Red Army soldiers taking a vast quantity of salt from a stationary railway wagon. He found himself arrested, hit with rifle butts and held in a cold cell for five days with little food and no blankets. On his release, without charge, he was diagnosed by a police doctor as having suffered a nervous breakdown because of his treatment. He could not speak of it without crying. An English version of his sworn statement finished up on Wilcox's desk, and another 16 civilians made statements on the promise that their names would not be passed on to the Soviets. Wilcox confessed to feeling quite impotent in dealing with such issues. The case of the Bottolis, husband and wife, left him with similar feelings, and in this case the events were all situated in the British Zone.

Paul and Maria Bottoli were in their early 50s. He was a master chimney sweep and she owned a garage attached to their house at Simmeringer Hauptstrasse 5 in *Bezirk* 11. Mrs Bottoli allowed various local firms to park their vehicles in the garage. She also agreed to the request of a local man, Viktor Kubitschek, who asked permission to park a car there that he drove for the Soviet Central Kommandatura. On the night of 13-14 February 1946 someone opened the garage, apparently with a key since there was no sign of a forced entry, and stole the Soviet car. As soon as he knew that the car was missing Kubitschek told Mrs Bottoli. She advised him to inform the police; which he did. Early that afternoon a group of Red Army soldiers turned up at the Bottolis' house and asked them to accompany them to the Central Kommandatura. After about an hour Mrs Bottoli was told that she could go home. She asked what would happen to her husband and was told that he could 'rot' in custody unless she produced 25,000 *Schillings*. In her deposition she stated that she was also warned that she also could be locked up and that everything would be taken from her. The Soviets refused every request from the British to let them have Mr Bottoli, or even to interview him. They also ignored the fact that everything that they had done was in contravention of the Arrest Agreement. After four days they compelled the Bottolis to sign a document giving the Soviets a car, even though first, the Bottolis could not afford one; second, the original car had been recovered across the border in Hungary and the man driving it arrested; and third, that the Viennese notary called in to prepare the document had said that it was illegal. Wilcox's protests as head of the British Public Safety Branch, and those of his superiors, got nowhere.

Russian commanders knew, or had no excuse for not knowing, where the British *Bezirke* began and ended, although they objected strongly to one of Wilcox's local commanders sending two armoured cars and a squad of Military Police to deal with Red Army troops reported as robbing a train which had stopped at a station in the British Zone. The Soviet General Lebenko wanted 'severe disciplinary action' taken against the British officer involved. Wilcox thought he was now in a position 'to write back a snorter.'

A few days later Wilcox was on his way to dinner when he was told that a British officer had been arrested by the Soviets for entering their zone outside the city. He spent two and a half hours on the phone trying to get some details. In the end, despairing that he never got any satisfaction from the Soviets, he threatened to call their general; it was only then that he was told that while the officer had been held for six hours, he had already been released.

If their officers should have known better, it may well have been that the ordinary Red Army soldiers who wanted to get from one part of the Soviet Zone to another and were not clear that the British were in the way; there was a further complication in that, until the beginning of 1946, Red Army soldiers still occupied barracks and billets in the British Zone.

Finally, there was the problem emanating from the involvement of Red Army soldiers in the black market. The Viennese police estimated that they were involved in at least 70 percent of it; two areas in *Bezirk* 4, Nachsmarkt and Resselpark, in the Soviet Zone but wedged between two British districts, were particularly notorious. Red Army soldiers were often left to their own devices to find billets and they still engaged in looting. Even though the Soviet authorities did admit to the problems and had begun to seek to restore some order and discipline, they insisted that their Allies speak of offenders not as Red Army soldiers but as men wearing the uniform of the Red Army. At first Wilcox strengthened the Viennese police by having two armoured cars available to back them up, though he doubted that armoured cars were much use other than as a very general deterrent to disorderly behaviour. In February 1946, however, he managed to arrange for a Provost Battery to be formed from men in the Essex Yeomanry then stationed in the city. The Battery consisted of five sections, one for each of the British *Bezirke*. Each section had an N.C.O. and sixteen other ranks. They were given a series of lectures on police duties by Major Charles Noble, a former station sergeant of the Metropolitan Police, and they patrolled the streets on foot or in jeeps alongside Viennese police officers.

As elsewhere, the soldiers of the different Allies confronted and fought each other over a variety of perceived slights and rivalries. One Sunday evening in June 1946, near to the Schönbrunn Palace, a group of Red Army soldiers decided to joke about the kilts of a group of Argyll and Sutherland Highlanders. They rapidly found that they had chosen the wrong men to mock and in the ensuing affray a Red Army lieutenant was killed. The offender was identified, arrested, court martialled and sentenced to death. The Russian commander was satisfied, though he expected a summary execution. Summary executions, however, were not the British way. The soldier appealed and Wilcox offered to travel to London to give evidence about the lawless behaviour of the Red Army and the provocation offered. He was assured by the military authorities, however, that his presence was not required since there was already sufficient evidence to ensure a reprieve.

Tangentially, it is worth mentioning that, when he saw something that he thought was wrong, Wilcox was fully prepared to interfere in the Soviet Zone. In January 1946, for example, he wrote to Ethel about such an incident. He stopped at a railway station in the Soviet Zone where he had heard of some 3,000 people, mainly women and children, who had been thrown out of Yugoslavia because they were Germans:

> The Russians have now washed their hands of them and left them in the railway trucks where they have been for several days. At least one has died and many are ill. Quite a number have drifted into Vienna where we fear they may spread disease. So we have had to put a police guard on them and tomorrow we shall move them into a British Displaced Persons Camp. I felt rather sorry for them all standing about in the snow and I was glad to get back in the car and hurry back to the mess for tea.

The Red Army was Wilcox's principal military problem, but as a police officer and temporary military gentleman he had several awkward moments with senior regular officers of the British Army. Wilcox saw it as a police officer's duty to assess a situation, use his discretion and act accordingly; his commanding general in Vienna, a Guards officer, in contrast believed that military discipline required obedience to orders passed down through the chain of command.

First came Wilcox's decision to attend the funeral of a young Viennese police officer killed in the line of duty. Given that he worked so closely with the local police, Wilcox thought he really ought to do this and he attended with Captain Greenhill and three staff members; they marched behind the coffin and stood at the graveside where several speeches were made. Unfortunately for Public Safety/Military relations, Wilcox did this without reference to the general; and the newspaper photographs of Wilcox and his men walking behind the coffin only served to aggravate matters. The general was displeased; first, he had not been consulted, and second, any decision about marching in a funeral parade was his to make.

Wilcox had been critical of the use of Italian police for domestic duties and he issued instructions to the Police President in Vienna that his men were not to be employed in such tasks by British Army Officers. The general was incensed, believing that if anyone was to have issued such an order, it should have been him.

The most serious clash with the general, however, came early on when, in November 1945, the Austrians held a general election and when it was proposed to hold a procession through Vienna. At that moment, the British were in command of the international zone and the British general instructed the police to prevent any procession from taking place. The general felt that he could rely upon a proclamation then in force forbidding any demonstrations. Wilcox, however, feared that any such ban was likely to create the problem that the general was anxious to avoid. In what appears to have been a tense meeting, Wilcox warned that since the procession had already been announced, any attempt to stop it might lead to trouble. The general dug his heels in. Wilcox then warned further that, if there was serious disorder, the police might call upon the assistance of British troops; if they were compelled to fire on the crowd it would not look good for the British and there would have to be an enquiry. He offered to put his advice in writing which, it appeared, was totally alien to the military mind of the period. The general rejected the idea of having anything in writing but he did not order the prevention of electoral processions or demonstrations and, in the event, everything passed off peacefully. In retrospect, Wilcox felt that he could have behaved with more tact and discretion towards the general than he did, but soldiering was the general's job and policing was Wilcox's.

Vienna: Crime and Police

The black market was probably the biggest crime problem that confronted Wilcox, his Public Safety officers and the Viennese police in the year following the end of the war. He did not doubt that British and American troops were involved but, generally, this appears to have been in a personal capacity dealing with relatively small exchanges. The French appeared to be relatively circumspect, but rather more engaged; and, as noted earlier, black marketeering was rampant among all ranks of the Red Army.

In November 1945, following a tip-off and the discovery of 100 sacks of sugar and over one and a half million Schillings, a careful watch was maintained of a house in *Bezirk* 5. Eventually, three lorries arrived loaded with sugar. The Red Army captain in command of the convoy could not account for the sugar, and he and his three drivers were handed over to the Soviet authorities. The evidence unearthed suggested an elaborate transaction involving Russians, Czechoslovaks and some Viennese merchants; it was passed to the Soviet War Prosecutor's Department.

Like these Viennese merchants, other Viennese were involved in significant black market offences. An Austrian official in the Central Food Office, for example, drew a large number of ration cards and sold them on the black market; eight people, including two Greeks, were brought before an Austrian court for involvement in this offence.

Yet most of the black market, in so far as it involved Austrians and the Red Army, appears to have been concerned with foodstuffs and the lack of ready money among the Viennese. Many people were desperate. Wilcox chose to help a friend of his interpreter, who lacked money to feed and clothe herself and her two children, and whose husband was a prisoner of war in the Soviet Union. The husband was an artist; Wilcox visited her house and bought a painting of a Finnish snow scene for 25 *Schillings*. Since he had no need of his cigarette ration he gave her cigarettes which, in much of war-ravaged Europe, were more valuable than cash. Most of the Red Army soldiers engaged in the bartering in Naschmarkt and Resselpark were initially interested in exchanging cigarettes and foodstuffs; the former came mainly from the Balkans and the latter from the countryside under Soviet control, but also from Hungary. They exchanged these for bicycles, jewellery and watches; but as time went on they seem to have become more interested in acquiring civilian clothing. Also, as the New Year dawned, the Soviet authorities began to get a greater grip on Red Army behaviour and the open black markets of Naschmarkt and Resselpark came under pressure; the surrounding streets, however, still provided a venue for bartering.

In addition to the black market there were the more usual problems for the police of traffic regulations, occasional demonstrations that appeared to threaten public order, and crime. In his report for the month of February 1946, Wilcox regretted that 'drivers, Allied and Austrian, vie with pedestrians in ignoring elementary traffic precautions.' The roads were still damaged by the fighting and by tracked vehicles, and a high percentage of the vehicles on the streets were the property of the Allies, but the numbers of deaths and injuries were alarming. In October 1945, for example, 140 people were killed or injured by military vehicles and another 46 by civilian vehicles; in just over a quarter of these incidents, the driver failed to stop. The Military Police of all four powers were concerned and met regularly to consider how best the problem might be resolved, since the Viennese police had no jurisdiction over Allied military personnel. Again, members of the Red Army were identified as the principal culprits; in November, for example, out of 57 hit and run incidents, Soviet soldiers were identified as responsible for 44.

In spite of the shortages, the winter cold and the hunger there were no demonstrations in protest over the situation. Perhaps the Viennese feared how the Red Army in particular would respond. There were, however, parades and rallies that it was felt required some police supervision. There were, as noted above, political rallies before the election of November 1945. There were others to celebrate liberation, to demand the incorporation of South Tyrol into the Austrian Republic, and to demand that Jews be allowed to travel and settle in Palestine. None created problems.

In the matter of crime, Wilcox recognised that there were problems with the statistics but he also believed that the scale of significant theft was confused in the first sets of statistics that he received from the police. Many Viennese had left the city early in 1945 and only discovered break-ins on their return, and hence sometimes long after they had happened. It appeared also that many victims were reluctant to report a theft because they were afraid of the occupying troops and of deserters who may have been responsible, and because they believed that the police either could not or would not take any action. Although crimes of violence were always fewer than crimes against property, there appeared to be a high level of violence in post-war Vienna. It did not reach the levels faced in the south of Italy with its brigand tradition and the numbers of deserters that linked with or fought with them, but it was greater than that faced at home by British police officers. Wilcox attempted a comparison with the much bigger metropolis of London and found murder and violence to be significantly greater in the Austrian capital. Again, as in Italy, soldiers and deserters were involved; the Red Army in particular was notorious for the way in which it made free use of its guns.

In January 1946 three men began molesting civilians in the French Zone and firing pistols. The Viennese police pursued them; one was shot and killed and the other two, still with the police in pursuit, entered the British Zone where there was another exchange of shots. One of the two was killed, the other was arrested. Subsequently all three were identified as Russian, though they may have been the gang, or part of the gang, that was believed to be French and that had been creating problems for a month or so. The following July, a Red Army officer was entertained by a Viennese couple in the British *Bezirk* 11; he got very drunk, shot dead the husband and wounded the wife. Arrests conducted by Soviet troops, as in the case of Franz Sverak, commonly involved the use of rifle butts. Yet civilian criminals were also fully prepared to use guns, possibly because there were so many available at the end of the war.

Table 1: Offences by Allied Troops reported by the Viennese Police January to August 1946

	Jan	Feb	Mar	Apr	May	Jun	Jul	Aug
British	2	1	2	3	7	3	6	1
American	13	5	23	6	17	9	20	24
French	18	23	48	17	18	9	9	6
Soviet	210	133	119	70	102	78	60	45

The Red Army soldiers were also notorious for assaults on women. Wilcox recalled an incident towards the end of August 1945 on a crossing point from the British Zone of Austrian Styria into the neighbouring Soviet Zone. Two Red Army soldiers stopped two young women, aged 19 and 22, and the fiancé of one of them, even though all three held the appropriate passes signed by the respective British and Soviet headquarters. The soldiers tore up the passes. The two women were taken into a wood and raped; the young man was held in custody for four days. The British authorities sent a full report to their Soviet counterparts, but a month later had received no reply. They also ceased to issue any passes to Austrian women unless they travelled in British vehicles.

The incidence of rape, as elsewhere during and immediately after the war, is difficult to assess because of the reluctance of victims to come forward. The Red Army has acquired a bad reputation for its treatment of women in Germany, especially the units under the command of Marshal Malinovsky, and it was units of Malinovsky's army that were among the first to enter Vienna. Some have suggested

70,000 to 100,000 rapes by Red Army soldiers in the city, with some women being victimised more than once.

In the summer of 1945, Austrian doctors were reported to be carrying out abortions to terminate 'war-related pregnancies', many of which were the result of rape. Yet the statistics of reports to the Vienna Police and passed to the Public Safety Committee gave a tiny level of reported rapes; a total of 30 in August 1945, 21 in September and 39 in October. The next set of statistics are fragmentary, to the extent that the statistics in Wilcox's minutes of the meetings cover only five of the months between February and August 1946, but they do provide the allegation of where the attackers came from. Thus, in February, there were seven rapes with the perpetrators identified as five Soviets and two Austrians; in April 11 rapes, five involving Soviets and five Austrians; in May, 17 involving seven Soviets, one Frenchman and three Austrians; in June, six, involving six Soviets and one Austrian; in August, seven, involving one Soviet, 2 Americans and five Austrians.

Yet again, the statistics offer problems. On 24 February 1946, for example, Wilcox recorded the arrest of a Red Army soldier for rape who was then handed over to the Soviet authorities. Possibly as a result of a continuing fear among the police of upsetting the Soviets, Wilcox noted that 'the official police record placed [the soldier] in the category "of unknown nationality"'.

In addition to rapes and other sexual assaults, the desperation of many women led them to sell themselves to soldiers. This, in turn, meant that once again as they had done elsewhere, British police officers found themselves involved in the some kind of brothel and prostitute vetting, as had been common across Europe for well over a century. In the monthly report of the Public Safety Branch for January 1946, for example, it was noted that 50 women had been taken into custody and medically examined; 32 were found to have venereal disease, six were still awaiting the outcome of their examination, and the remaining 12 were free from any disease. At the same time, in what must have produced echoes of his time in Gerald Road, a hotel in *Bezirk* 12 was found to be used by Allied troops as a brothel and a raid on 30 January found eight French and five British soldiers with 14 women, of whom nine were infected. It is important to note at this point that the statistics for V.D. infection soared in the early months of occupation, which may also be a reflection of the incidence of rape.

The small number of Civil Affairs officers making up the Public Safety Branches of all four powers and their Military Police were never sufficient to police the whole of Vienna, and none of the Allies had any intention of permanently employing their soldiers to do so. The British, for example, had just 179 Redcaps in Vienna – a Provost Company, a Traffic Company and a section of S.I.B., the corps' detective branch. The British provost company appear to have acted as a deterrent to Red Army soldiers wandering in the British sector, even though they had only 68 men to deploy on patrols. These were backed up by the armoured cars obtained by Wilcox and his Provost Battery but, technically, none of these had any authority over Soviet soldiers, though his successful request for English-speaking Soviet soldiers to accompany his men sometimes when on patrol probably helped.

On the eve of the war there were about 10,000 police in Vienna. Wilcox's enquiries suggested that most of the senior officers in the uniform branch were Germans, while their juniors were mainly 'pro-Nazi Austrian officers and N.C.O.s … given promotion after receiving a course of training in Berlin.' The numbers appeared similar when the western Allies arrived; but the evidence collected by the Public Safety Branch suggested a large number of recalled pensioners and auxiliaries:

Table 2: Strength of Viennese Police, September 1945

	Uniform	Criminal	Administration	Total
Regulars	1,790	187	993	2,970
Recalled pensioners	772	39	94	905
Auxiliaries	3,667	297	1,558	5,522
Total	**6,229**	**523**	**2,645**	**9,397**

But there were problems here. Wilcox reckoned that 80 percent of the police needed training and that there were too many involved in administrative duties. Moreover, the ground area of the city had expanded, leading to an increase in the number of *Bezirke* from 21 on the outbreak of war to 26. Much of the new districts were not yet built up, but they still required some police presence.

The main difficulty that Wilcox faced initially, however, stemmed from the Soviet occupation. He stressed his impression that the Soviets had a very different view of policing; they 'regard the police as a political instrument rather than an impartial body for protecting the public against disorder and crime.'

When the Red Army occupied the city there were no police to be found on the streets for some time. Gradually, a few men drifted back to their police stations and were allowed to take up their duties again, provided they could demonstrate that they had possessed no Nazi sympathies. The Soviets then appointed Rudolf Hautmann as commander of what they termed the *Hilfspolizei*. Hautmann was a tram driver with no police experience, but he was a good Communist. *Hilfspolizei* commanders were appointed to the *Bezirke* and, again, Communist Party membership or sympathy was the main recommendation for the job.

These commanders appointed their own men using the same criteria; it was estimated by the P.S.B. officers of the western Allies that no more than 20 percent of the police in the *Bezirke* had any police experience when they arrived. Wilcox found three of the local police commanders in the British Zone to be lacking in experience and undesirable: a stage-hand, a locksmith and a tool-maker with criminal convictions for theft, fraud and assault. He had all three removed in September, and a fourth in October.

But difficulties remained, since Austrian Communists and Socialists were keen to ensure that senior police appointments were political rather than based on police experience and expertise. Just over two weeks before the Austrian election of November 1945, an agreement was reached between senior Austrian Communists and Socialists to ensure that such remained the case; and Wilcox was both shocked and annoyed to see Communist Party posters reading: 'We must never allow the police to get into the hands of the reactionaries again. Therefore vote for the Communist Party of Austria.'

The Austrian People's Party won the election with just under 50 percent of the vote but its leader, Leopold Figl, decided to maintain the tripartite grand coalition of his party, the Socialists and the Communists which had run the country since the end of the war. The Communists, with only five percent of the vote, got only one cabinet post, but their agreement with the Socialists on senior police appointments was maintained and Wilcox fumed at the way in which experienced officers continued to be replaced by political placemen with the western Allies sitting back and doing nothing. He noted, for example, the replacement of the police chief of *Bezirk* 3 in April 1946. Franz Schupp, the man replaced, was a professional police officer with 26 years' service and legal qualifications; his replacement, a nominee of the Socialist Party, was a civil service clerk with no police or legal experience. Wilcox's complaints to the Ministry of the Interior were ignored.

In the same month, the head of the personnel bureau of the uniform branch, a professional police officer who had been in post for many years, was replaced by a Communist who had joined the police as an auxiliary in May 1945 when he was yet to acquire Austrian citizenship. Fortunately, the men at the top of the Vienna Police, at least in Wilcox's eyes, had a clear-eyed vision of how police officers should behave and where their loyalties ought to be.

A series of senior appointments had been made and approved by the Soviet authorities shortly before the western Allies arrived. Wilcox and his deputy, John 'Jock' Reid, met Ignaz Pamer, the Police President, and Max Pammer, the head of the Political and Intelligence Department, and considered that they were unlikely to find two better or more suitable men:

> [They] appear to be aware of the danger of the police becoming a political instrument and are sympathetic towards our desire to construct an impartial and efficient Police Force.

After the unification of Austria with Germany in 1938 Pammer had lost his post and spent three years in the concentration camp at Dachau.

Ignaz Pamer made a particular impact on Wilcox. He described him as 'a charming and cultivated gentleman of the old school.' Old school was right. Pamer had 35 years' experience with the police. He had been Police President of Vienna and had retired some years before the *Anschluss*. He was recalled from retirement in the summer of 1945, aged 79. His knowledge and experience was vast. Wilcox was concerned about the policing arrangements when the British authorities decided to stage a Military Tattoo in the grounds of the Schönbrunn Palace. Pamer reassured him, not least by recalling the plans that he had made at the beginning of the century for a visit by Edward VII.

Given his age, it was hardly surprising that Pamer was replaced in 1946, just under a year after his reappointment. It was equally hardly surprising, though unfortunate, that his replacement was a political appointee. The British P.S.O.s gave the old man two inscribed silver tankards as an indication of the high standing in which they held him. Wilcox himself had already given him a copy of Robert Graves's *I Claudius*, a book which had originally been published ten years earlier and which Pamer had said he was very keen to read.

Max Pammer was also replaced by a political appointee, but he continued to have an influential position in the Ministry of the Interior and from here he kept Wilcox and Reid informed of the activities of Communist and Socialist politicians.

A third senior man restored to his old post was Heinrich Hüttl, who had been Commandant of the Vienna Police Training School before the Nazi takeover and who, like Pammer, had spent several years in a Nazi concentration camp. In August 1946 Hüttl made a radio broadcast in support of his vision of the Viennese Police in which he explained that they should behave decently towards both their comrades and the public. He expected an officer to be 'friendly, polite, not overbearing ... a servant of the democratic republic.' Hüttl sent a translation to Wilcox, who was then back as a civilian police officer in England. It was exactly the kind of police officer that Wilcox had hoped to see created for the city; indeed, it was the kind of police force that some senior figures in Britain believed could save future conflict in the world.

The late 1930s had seen the first of Charles Reith's glowing histories of the English Police in which he praised their distinctiveness, arguing that they were an institution that came from the people as opposed to those on continental Europe that were imposed by government. At the end of 1943 Herbert Morrison, the Home Secretary in the wartime coalition, spoke in praise of the 'high standard of orderliness' which had developed in the British Isles since the late eighteenth century and which had developed alongside the unique system of policing. The hope was that establishing such police across Europe in the wake of war would prevent future conflict. From the moment that he entered Vienna, Wilcox thought it important to create a police system with many of the attributes of the British system, and he and his small group of British P.S.O.s, all former British police officers, made this a top priority. On 25 August 1945, for example, he drafted a report on the Viennese Police and their immediate needs. The minutes of the Four Power meeting that General Travnikov chaired on 8 September clearly suggest that the British were the driving force behind police reorganisation and training in the city.

The Viennese Police were considered by Wilcox to have a series of problems, some concerning their relationship with the public and the kind of men recruited, but many more concerning equipment. The Public Safety Commission met monthly and the progress of the Viennese Police was always a key item on the agenda. At an initial meeting on 24 September 1945 it was agreed, probably on British prompting, that the public's lack of confidence in the police was the result of the police officers' lack of training and integrity, and the preparedness to use arbitrary methods emanating from political considerations.

The Nazi officers had all gone, but it was suggested that some of the men labelled as *Anwärter*[4] in the Nazi Party might been retained. The situation on the ground, however, revealed that dubious practices that may have their origins in the Nazi period were now being exercised against former Nazis and others. There were allegations, for example, 'of police detaining persons without trial, of sending them to forced labour, of evicting people from houses and seizing their furniture, and of forcing unwilling Poles, Czechs and others to return to their countries.'

Perhaps the Viennese had not realised, but the anti-Nazi legislation deployed in Vienna was deployed principally by the Political Police (Staatspolizei), a force of some 600 who were not responsible to officers in the *Bezirke* but directly to a Communist political appointee, Dr. Heinrich Dürmayer. In a document marked 'secret', Wilcox noted that Dürmayer had a law degree, but he had also served as a major in the International Brigades in Spain, had spent time in Moscow and was now a member of the Central Executive of the Communist Party:

'He pays little attention to the Police President or to his superiors at the Central Police Direction of the Ministry of the Interior. [He] deals directly with the Austrian Communist Party and with the Russians.'

Dürmayer freely admitted to the Public Safety Committee that before any legislation had been passed, he had made it up as he thought fit. Wilcox had little time for Dürmayer and his political police, though it was admitted in the minutes of the September meeting that some of the people responsible for seizing furniture were British officers who had leaned upon members of a new housing department to acquire certain things for messes and billets.

The problem of the lack of integrity and of the arbitrary behaviour by ordinary police officers was, it was believed, something that could be solved by training. It was also agreed that the police should

---

4   The Nazi Party had an extensive and complex system of ranks. *Anwärter* was the lowest of these, and referred to someone who had been accepted into a government position; but there were two kinds: those who were already Party members and those who were not. The word might be translated as 'applicant' or 'candidate'.

be regarded as a single force for the entire city and not organised and trained separately in the four different zones. This was a British proposal to which the Americans and the French quickly agreed, and the Soviets a little more slowly. A single force, however, meant that there had to be a single training school; the pre-war school in *Bezirk* 3 had been destroyed during the conflict so somewhere new was essential.

Rossauer Barracks, which was in *Bezirk* 9 in the American Zone, was agreed upon as the new training school; the difficulty here was that when it was selected for its new role, it was occupied by members of the Red Army and it took some weeks to get them to move, after which the building had to be cleaned and prepared for its new role.

Equipment problems were sorted by the Allies working together effectively and in what appears to have been a genuine spirit of co-operation. There was a petrol shortage that lasted for longer than some of the other problems, but this appears to have originated in a misunderstanding between two Austrian ministries, that of Reconstruction and that of the Interior.

It was agreed to re-establish the city's mounted police; a number of former police horses were in the American Zone of the country around Linz, and the Soviets agreed to find fodder for the horses from Lower Austria. On a Soviet recommendation, initially opposed by the French, it was agreed to raise the food ration for the police; in the end it was considered that this might provide an incentive for a better standard of recruit. Uniforms were lacking; it was hoped that the police would be back in their pre-war green tunics and black trousers with a red stripe during the summer of 1946, but until then it was a case of make-do and mend. There were attempts to get old Wehrmacht uniforms, but they were found to be poor of quality and liable to shrink; some men took to the streets in boots and battledress, much of which was a mixture of British or Italian origin. A large number of overcoats, which were regarded as essential for the winter, were supplied by the Americans.

At the end of the war Colonel Gordon Halland, the first Commandant at Hendon, became one of the leading figures of the British Zone of Germany. He was extremely reluctant to see the German police rearmed. This does not appear to have been a concern to Wilcox in Vienna. In September 1945 it was minuted that there were firearms available for just under two-thirds of the patrolmen and detectives, and these weapons were a mixture of German, Austrian, Italian, French and Soviet rifles and pistols. Wilcox went along with his Allies, all of whom were used to having armed police officers at home; and the standardisation of police weaponry gradually developed. Key in his acceptance of the idea of an armed police was his recognition that the British Army could not, and he thought should not, be regularly employed as an armed back-up for police on the streets of the British Zone. Moreover, he was well aware of how dangerous it was for police officers on patrol throughout the city. In his radio broadcast of August 1946, Hüttl told his listeners that over the last 15 months, 13 police probationers had lost their lives in fighting criminals.

Nor was it only the streets that were potentially dangerous for the Viennese Police; so was the territory under the ground. As anyone familiar with Graham Greene's novella and Carol Reed's film *The Third Man* will know, Vienna had a fine, large sewer system. This dated back to the early eighteenth century, was expanded during the nineteenth, though the plans for further extension collapsed with the financial problems following the First World War. There appears to have been some concern in 1945 that the tunnels might become a haven for refugees, displaced persons and fugitive Nazis. But natives of Vienna probably knew that, while the sewers might be a way of moving secretly – always useful for those involved in major black market enterprise like Greene's Harry Lime - they were not the best of places in which to hide for any length of time. A particularly wide tunnel with a broad edge stretching for two kilometres might have looked like somewhere that a large group of people could rest and keep out of sight, but a heavy rainstorm unheard by people in the sewer could lead to the tunnel flooding rapidly and to the disappearance of the narrow exit under fast flowing water.

Nevertheless, a special detachment of eighteen police officers was recruited to patrol the 2,400 kilometres of the sewer system; they had their own special police station and Wilcox promised to take a BBC producer there to make a broadcast. As might be expected given their working conditions, this detachment indented for soap, disinfectant, powerful lamps and other materiel that they required for their unique and smelly task.

Before the war Viennese police officers underwent two-years of training, following a curriculum ranging widely from the Criminal and the Civil Law, to Youth Welfare, traffic duty, and to various regulations applying to, amongst other things, markets and places of entertainment such as cinemas and theatres.

He was required to be an Austrian citizen of unblemished character, aged between 20 and 34 years, well-built, at least 1.68 metres tall, a good ability in writing reports in the German language and either unmarried or a widower without children. The Public Safety Commission agreed that recruiting men of this standard should be the ultimate aim; they were prepared to have former members of the police, even those who had served in the Wehrmacht, and there was continuing debate over those designated as *Anwärters* under the Nazi regime.

The British began training men in their *Bezirke* shortly before the end of August. It was planned to have nearly 300 potential patrolmen undergoing courses of three months by early November, two months before the Rossauer School was ready. The Criminal Police were also given a three-month course, but this was at the Police Headquarters. Wilcox was not one of those whose romantic vision of the British police denied that they employed political investigators; he thought this a necessity of every police institution and considered the British Special Branch to be such. Yet he doubted that Dürmayer's men received any proper training about the wider police role; they were, he believed, almost entirely members of the Communist party upholding Soviet ideology and the Soviet perception of police.

Rossauer Police Training School was opened on 18 January 1946 in the presence of Chancellor Figl and his Minister of the Interior.

Wilcox was on the podium to welcome them, along with three other British officers including Major Noble, one of his *Bezirk* commanders.

Yet Wilcox was still looking to his civilian future. Jock Reid had acted in his place for much of November and December as Wilcox first was admitted to hospital for a couple of weeks – in the usual monthly report Reid did not say what his problem was - and then he travelled back to England under the scheme known as L.I.A.P. The acronym stood for Leave in Addition to Python; Python being the name for posting home troops who had served abroad for four years or more. L.I.A.P. was introduced in 1944 to permit leave for those who had served abroad for two years and nine months. Wilcox appears to have benefited from a slightly liberal stretching of his period overseas, though the extension may have been in part convalescence.

Pastimes and Prisons

While Wilcox had more freedom than most to move around the city, there were restrictions. The city was in the middle of the Soviet Zone of Austria, and travel beyond the city limits required authority, though he does not appear to have been aware of this initially.

Shortly after his arrival in Vienna he felt that he could telephone Ethel; after all, the war was over and it did not seem to be a secret now as to where he was. He urged her to come and visit, and to bring some of the best post-war currency, in other words, cigarettes that could be given to those who looked after him or otherwise helped. Ethel was keen to see him again and, collecting a large box of cigarettes containing smaller cartons, she set off to travel, catching a train from Paris. But it was in Paris that her problems began, and the cigarettes began to prove their use. The customs officer inspecting her bags commented on the very large number of cigarettes, but was satisfied with the gift of a carton.

The Thomas Cook Office in Paris refused to sell her a ticket on the grounds that she had no *laissez passer rouge* (authorisation to travel). She went to the ticket office in the railway station from which the trains left for Vienna and successfully bought a ticket.

As the train departed the ticket inspector asked to see her *laissez passer rouge*; a carton of cigarettes led to a shrug of the shoulders; he came back later for more.

On the train Ethel was fortunate to make the acquaintance of a young French woman who had been in the Resistance and who was heading east to find her husband, who had been a P.O.W. The French woman and her friends organised a distraction as the train went through the American Zone of Austria so that the American soldier did not get round to looking at Ethel's passport and finding her lack of a *laissez passer*.

No-one appears to have bothered her, or demanded to see anything in the British Zone. The final sector crossed by the train was that of the Soviets. Possibly encouraged by the British laxity, Ethel had been prepared to admit that she had no travel papers, but her new-found French friends would have none of it. They were already aware of the Red Army's propensity for rape and they arranged for her to squeeze into the crack between the carriage wall and the top bunk of the wagon lit; the bunk was then occupied by a French woman and the Red Army train inspector only saw her, her passport and her travel permit as she lay next to the squashed Ethel.

Ethel stayed in Vienna for two weeks. Wilcox was slightly worried about her journey back and he did not think it would be possible to pull any strings by having her mention his name. Once again, Ethel's new friend from the French Resistance came to her aid. As she waited on Vienna station she saw a young boy with a placard stating 'Lady Wilcox.' She was still laughing about this fifty years later. The youth took her to the Resistance woman, who explained that she had arranged for her to travel with two men, one of whom had papers for his girlfriend who was running an art exhibition and which had been extended for two weeks so that she could not travel back with him. Wilcox jokingly told her to 'enjoy' herself, and she was able to travel home without mentioning his name.

Once Ethel had gone, Wilcox had to find other ways to pass any spare time that he could squeeze from his duties. He does not appear to have been so eager to squeeze such time when he was alone with his comrades, but as soon as the Mounted Police were given back their horses Wilcox began to borrow one so as to ride in the park of the Schönbrunn Palace and the much bigger Prater with its celebrated big wheel, the *Wurstelprater*, on which Harry Lime dispensed his cynical perception of war and profiteering in *The Third Man*.

Much to the envy of the Americans and the French, the British had acquired the magnificent baroque Kinsky Palace and transformed it into their Officers Club. Reviving some of its pre-war splendour, the Kinsky provided dinner and cabaret. Vienna was a city that prided itself on its music, and almost as soon as the fighting stopped musicians were back on the streets and music venues reopened.

Wilcox also found the opportunity to extend his knowledge of opera and to extend the inauspicious start that he had made when looking for a suspect at Covent Garden under the tutelage of Sergeant Wyatt. He had already used his postings in Naples and Rome to see *Rigoletto* and *Tosca*. There had also been the opera in Paris and then, courtesy of an Australian singer performing in Vienna, he received tickets for Carmen. He regretted that he had still not seen the last three acts of *Aida* as a result of sitting in the pub with Wyatt; and, he confessed to Ethel, he was still not sure whether or not he really liked opera.

In addition to the police, the Public Safety officers were also responsible for the fire service. Generally Wilcox had little involvement, or even interest in this area; the senior American officer, after all, had a fire service background. However, it was the fire service element of his role that enabled him to visit Paris and to spend yet more time with Ethel.

The officer responsible for the fire service in the French *Bezirke* received an invitation to attend an international conference on Fire Prevention early in 1946. He extended the invitation to his American and British counterparts. The American officer chose to drive in his own car with his attractive Austrian secretary. He was extremely annoyed when officials at the French frontier insisted that she be sprayed with disinfectant, but Paris made up for it. He turned up at the opening ceremony with the secretary, but was not seen again at the conference. The pair appear to have passed their time seeing the sites, and there was a certain amount of comment about what else they might have been doing.

Wilcox and Bill Balance, a former Metropolitan Police Inspector, agreed to travel with the French officer in a car for which he showed the same affection as Wilcox did for his Fiat. Unfortunately the Frenchman's car did not have the same hardiness and resilience. Extremely late, and chugging at about 15 miles an hour, the car limped into Tübingen, where the French army had established its German headquarters. A meal appears to have been found and the car was taken in for repair. The following morning they set off for Paris, but well before their arrival the mechanical fault reoccurred. They made the opening of the conference travel-stained, tired and not a little put-out, with an hour to spare.

Even though a senior officer of the French Fire Service (*les Sapeurs-Pompiers*) had provided Wilcox and Ethel with an apartment, which she had reached some time before him, he took his attendance at the conference seriously. He and Bill Balance conscientiously attended every session, which was probably no bad thing since they had to assuage the fury of the Colonel of the *Sapeurs-Pompiers*. Like the *Gendarmerie*, the French Fire Service was a military institution. What had incensed the Colonel was the address of the secretary of the British Fire Brigades Union who, like his comrades who were attending, was a Communist. He explained to the delegates the values of a trade union for such an organisation given the way that a union might negotiate better pay and conditions. While he did not say as much to the Colonel, Wilcox considered that anyone promoting an international conference at that time might have expected such an address from one or more delegates; after all, there were plenty in the west who admired the Soviet experiment and their wartime sacrifices, and who believed that the future lay with Communism.

Fortunately, the momentary tension at the conference did nothing to limit the hospitality, which included a banquet and a visit to the opera. Probably a little too soon for Wilcox, Ethel was heading back to the girls and he was heading back to Vienna. Yet while Wilcox's military service in Vienna may have been eased by opera, good food and occasional riding, for most of the citizens life was hard, and especially so for those who found themselves locked up as suspects or convicted of criminal offending, particularly when that offending was deemed political.

When the British arrived in Vienna they found a large number of individuals were being held in police cells without trial and often without charge. As elsewhere in liberated or occupied Europe, de-Nazification laws were passed, although not always with a clear definition of what was included, or how charges were to be formulated and tried. The Austrians began to experiment with *Volksgerichte* (People's Courts), established in the principal urban areas – Vienna, Graz, Linz and Innsbruck. Unfortunately, as elsewhere in Europe, people took the opportunity of the post-war chaos to denounce old enemies, who had not necessarily been Nazis, and even to denounce people whose apartments they coveted; an allegation could lead to the accused's arrest while the person responsible for the denunciation could move rapidly into the vacant dwelling.

Given the state of the police in the summer of 1945, and the need to re-organise the legal system in the wake of the Nazi defeat, the problems are not surprising. The improving police force appears to have alleviated the situation as far as conventional crime was concerned. The police cells were gradually emptied of those held for long periods with or without charge though, Wilcox lamented, it was never possible to act in accordance with the Austrian system as it was before the Anschluss and bring criminals before a court within 48 hours of being charged. Like the reformed police, the prison system was unified. The central prison was in the American sector, but there was a subsidiary building in the British *Bezirk* 5 and a Juvenile Reformatory in *Bezirk* 11 where Wilcox's men played a significant role in ensuring that outstanding cases were cleared and that a probation system was established.

There were three D.P. camps in the British Zone where, in the autumn of 1946, there was an outbreak of typhus. A police cordon was created around the camps to prevent people entering or leaving. 'The people here are so undernourished,' Wilcox told Ethel, 'that they could put up little resistance.'

If, however, the D.P. camps in Vienna were bad, there was one incarceration centre that was far worse.

Simmeringer Heide Camp was in *Bezirk* 11; it was established to house political offenders, and as a consequence it came under the remit of Dürmayer and his political police. Dürmayer had decided on his own initiative to use Labour Camps and it was noted that some two to three arrests were made in the British sector alone in September 1945.

On entering Simmeringer Heide, the British found it to be in an appalling state. The men in charge were political appointees and the guards were people who had been held in Nazi concentration camps. There was serious overcrowding and very little medical supervision or sanitary arrangements. Two inmates had been allowed to die without being seen by a doctor, let alone any provision for them to be sent to a hospital. Protests to Pamer led to the camp being removed from Dürmayer's fiefdom; an experienced police officer took over running the camp and improved medical and sanitary provisions were established. Yet for some time, complaints to the commanders in the British sector that holding political suspects without trial, even in an improved camp, could not be a permanent solution fell on deaf ears. Eventually it was agreed that no-one detained in the British Zone by the Austrians could be sent to labour camps in other sectors without the agreement of the British Public Safety branch; the fear in this case was that such individuals might be tortured or spirited away into another country. The British also supervised the investigation of those in the camp, gradually whittling down the numbers until, by July 1946, none remained.

Although many of the senior officers of the Viennese police with whom Wilcox and his subordinates dealt spoke highly of the British 'model' and of the ethos that it provided for their new officers, Wilcox remained concerned about the political element that remained and that experienced men continued to be replaced by political appointees. As 1946 wore on he became increasingly worried about the Public Safety Branch's inability to do anything about it or to stop what appeared to be its growth. The Minister of the Interior appeared determined to create a Socialist Police; 'he describes it as "Democratic"', explained Wilcox, who feared that this could provoke the creation of police forces by other political parties.

There appeared no chance of removing the Communist influence in the Political Police. At the same time, and equally serious, was a belief among the Austrian authorities in general that in serious situations, particularly with reference to incidents concerning public order, civilians were better equipped to deal with the situation than experienced police commanders. Perhaps here he was looking back to his own confrontation with a senior soldier over the use of the law in election rallies.

In spite of these worries Wilcox generally found the work in Vienna to be stimulating if exhausting – he confessed to Ethel that once or twice he had taken R.A.F. exhaustion pills.[5] He thought that the senior police officers in Vienna were grateful for the presence of him and his men. At least they had kept the Viennese police largely free from Soviet domination, and unlike the Italians they showed some sympathy with the reforms that were advocated and appeared keen to employ some British methods.

Yet the war was over, it was uncertain how long his post in Vienna would survive and a future in civvy street was constantly on his mind. For the third time he had appeared before an appointment committee at home. A Chief Constable who had served in the Metropolitan Police wrote a brief comment on the 19 officers that applied to Buckinghamshire for the position of Assistant Chief Constable. He suggested five for the interview, with Wilcox as the front-runner, commenting that he was

---

5   Benzedrine Sulphate in tablet form was one such, and so were Wakey-Wakey pills of caffeine that were most often issued to gunners serving in Bomber Command. These pills were not, however, used as frequently as used to be believed and it appears that the R.A.F. was concerned about their repeated use and the impact on aircrew.

> one of the best if not the best of the young officers now in the
> Metropolitan Police.... He is fully up to the job in Buckinghamshire;
> is of a charming personality and modest disposition and has a wife
> who is a most worthy counterpart.

A reference apparently from Arthur Young, since it describes Wilcox as 'my right hand' in Italy, was also glowing. It stressed his ability with administration and detailing schemes; though it noted his tendency to be over modest and 'a trifle too retiring' and the fact that 'in an interview he is not able to be forceful enough to give his interviewers a proper impression of his abilities.'

Buckinghamshire was a case of third time lucky; Wilcox was offered, and accepted, the post. He had one last fling in the shape of a few days in Venice, staying at an elegant hotel appropriated by the British Army for officers in transit; he noted that the Army had a 'flair for commandeering the most desirable buildings.'

He then exchanged his khaki for the usual demob suit, trilby and overcoat in advance of getting fitted for his new, blue Buckinghamshire uniform.

1. The Sea Horse, Bristol, now gone, where Wilcox's father spent many good times and much of his money.
@Hartley photographs from know your place website

2. The Prince of Wales with Lord Trenchard and Col. Halland opening the Police College Hendon,
31 May 1934. Wilcox is the tallest student third man from the right in the row to the left of the picture.

3. *Future leaders of the police. Taking a break from their training at Hendon.*
Wilcox is the man with the newspaper.

Below: 4. Mainly due to the weather there were no pictures of Wilcox's wedding. The photo is the first extant picture of him and Ethel taken in Paris in 1946.

Below: 5 and 6. Metropolitan Police beats were carefully plotted and timed. After Hendon Wilcox spent time in 'E' Division for which the 1930s Beat Book survives. The maps here show the spread of the beats across the division and the detail for No. 6 Beat which covered part of the Strand up to Garrick Street.

Courtesy Metropolitan Police

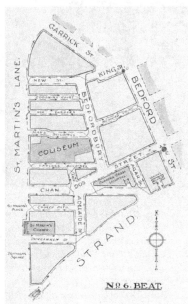

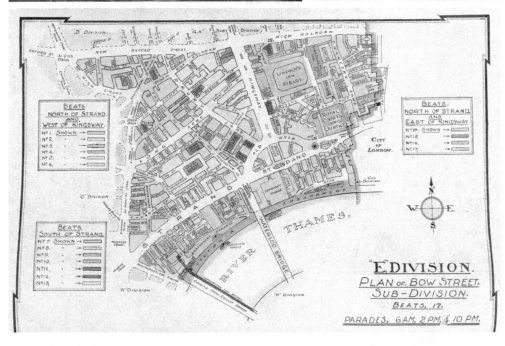

7 & 8. Italy 1944. Expecting to take about the training and preparedness of the Carabinieri for supporting the Allied Army, Wilcox found himself having to inspect them in all their best-dress finery, while he wore his British Army battledress after a long drive in a jeep that broke down.

9. Venice, Spring 1945. Taking the opportunity to ride a working gondola.

10 & 11. The Allied division of Austria and Vienna.

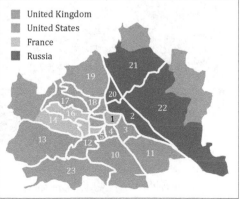

12. *January 1946, the opening of the Viennese Police Training School. From the left, Major Charles Noble (P.S.O.), Wilcox, Captain Kay (Army), Brigadier Verney (Army) shaking hands with the Austrian Chancellor.*

13. *British Public Safety Officers, Vienna, May 1946. Back row: Capt. T.W.M. Greenhill (Det. Sgt. Met); Capt. P.H. Bricknell (Station Sgt, Met); Capt. W.G. Horton (Gloucestershire Police); Capt. M.L. Turmer (Met); Capt. J. Madill (Sgt. Glasgow City). Front row: Major C. Noble (Station Sgt, Met); Major G.W. Brook (Inspector Bradford City); Lt. Col. Wilcox; Major J.C. ('Jock') Reid (Bradford City).*

14 & 15. Holiday in Switzerland 1949 with Stephen (note the English gentleman's dress), and skiing.

16. *Opening the bridge from the Girls' School to their playing field over the road, with his 'humorous' speech that upset many motor-cycle enthusiasts.*

17. In full dress as Chief Constable of Hertfordshire.

18. In retirement; morning coffee and newspaper in his garden.

CHAPTER 6

POST-WAR POLICING

Buckinghamshire Interval

Buckinghamshire was not the kind of place that Wilcox had experience of policing. It was largely rural. The county town was Aylesbury, with a population of around 25,000. There were two other significant urban areas. High Wycombe was slightly bigger; it was a centre of chair manufacture and during the war R.A.F. Bomber Command had established its headquarters there, while many of the chair makers found themselves making the bulk of the highly successful Mosquito fighter-bomber which, uniquely for the time, was principally made out of wood. Slough, about twice the size of Aylesbury and still in Buckinghamshire rather than Berkshire, had boomed during the inter-war period thanks to the work of the Slough Trading Estate and its provision for new estates and factories – factories that inspired John Betjeman to write before the war had begun:

> Come, friendly bombs and fall on Slough
> It isn't fit for humans now...

For the most part in 1946, 'urban' Buckinghamshire was still small market towns and villages, and these were quite different from the suburban districts of London that Wilcox had found rather dull in comparison with Bow Street and Chelsea. His wartime experience in Italy and his post-war role in Vienna, however, had given him maturity and an awareness of command, whatever the circumstances. Perhaps this was just as well, since he was left to his own devices when he arrived. He found six territorial divisions whose commanding superintendents appeared to know exactly what they were meant to be doing; and nobody appeared to be able to say what his predecessor had done, other than that he had taken a keen interest in the Boy Scout Movement.

The housing stock of the Buckinghamshire force was poor, and Colonel Thomas Warren, the Chief Constable, suggested that Wilcox start by building up the stock of police houses. This was a general problem at the end of the war; thousands of demobilised servicemen came home to find nowhere to live with new wives and families. Wilcox found an enthusiastic young architect who had recently been appointed to the County Council and who was keen to design the new police buildings. He and Wilcox even decided to seek the advice of police wives on the initial drawings; they then spent some time driving around the county looking for affordable and useable sites, probably the toughest part of the job.

It was not only junior police officers who required accommodation. Wilcox had difficulty in finding somewhere for himself, his wife and their young family. The Receiver of the Metropolitan Police was prepared to let Ethel and the girls stay in a police flat in Chelsea where Wilcox had been stationed before his army service, but the Receiver also stressed that this could not be for long as he needed the accommodation for his own force.

Wilcox stayed briefly in a room in the Bull's Head Hotel in Aylesbury, but even though he was relatively well-paid at £720 a year, this was only half of what he had been earning in the Army and insufficient to pay for the London flat and the Aylesbury hotel for long. After two weeks, Colonel Warren arranged for him to move to the Constitutional Club, where the caretaker and his wife provided him with meals. The problem here was that when the county assizes met, Wilcox had to leave for a week since the club served as the Judge's Lodgings.

The Buckinghamshire Standing Joint Committee recognised the problem, but every house that they found was deemed to be too expensive by the Home Office. Just before Christmas 1946 the opportunity arose to rent a house in the village of Chearsley, on a ridge some seven miles south-west of Aylesbury. Unfortunately the winter of 1946-47 was one of the worst in living memory. There was thick snow; there were power cuts and fuel was rationed. When the thaw came, things were no better for Wilcox; the roof leaked and the snow gave way to floods. In order to get to the Police Headquarters in Aylesbury Wilcox found himself having to wade across a flooded stream in thigh-high boots to be met by a police car on the far side.

Yet the floods also gave him a major task to work on. He spent several days in Slough, in a hastily-established operations room from where measures were co-ordinated with the Army, local government and the voluntary services to evacuate local residents of Wraysbury, who had been marooned by the flooding Thames.

As the Chief Constable's deputy, Wilcox found himself sent to greet Frederick Tarry, the new H.M. Inspector of Constabulary, when he came to make the annual inspection of 1947. Tarry was new to the job of Inspector but he had served as a Chief Constable since 1930, first in Exeter and then in Southampton. Wilcox approached the task with the memory of the pomp and circumstance that surrounded Dunning's visits to Bristol; but things had changed. Wilcox greeted Tarry in uniform, but there was no formal parade of the bulk of the force, no questioning of men carefully drilled in their answers, no ritualistic investigation of ledgers and other paperwork. Nor was there a formal tea with walnut cake. Wilcox showed Tarry into Colonel Warren's office where, to his surprise, the Colonel was dressed informally in country clothes. Wilcox was told to wait outside and the two senior men chatted for about an hour; he was then called back in, told that Tarry would like to visit one or two police stations and left to take him round. He later reflected: 'I do not think that Fred Tarry learnt much from the tutelage I was able to offer.'

Yet if there were some things that appeared to have changed

considerably since before the war, there were others redolent of the past.

When Wilcox had joined the Bristol City Police, John Watson, the Chief Constable, was investigated for using policemen and resources for his own benefit. There were also continual murmurings among constables throughout the English police service of harsh discipline and favouritism. When Wilcox arrived in Buckinghamshire he found Colonel Warren facing similar accusations.

Warren, like many county Chief Constables appointed in the inter-war years, had been a career soldier. He had been to Sandhurst, had served with distinction in the First World War, returned briefly to his native Ireland as a Resident Magistrate and become Chief Constable of Buckinghamshire in 1928. Shortly before Wilcox had arrived in Buckinghamshire, Warren had been accused of getting police officers to work on his farm. The accusation went nowhere, but a group of county councillors remained unhappy and brought further charges of maladministration before the Standing Joint Committee. During his first week in Buckinghamshire, Wilcox accompanied Warren to a difficult and tense meeting of the S.J.C., as the Chief Constable faced yet more accusations. Many of these appear to have originated in complaints by disgruntled members of the force; one committee member flourished a bundle of anonymous letters that he had received carrying accusations. Warren, it was claimed, had not been fair and impartial in authorising allowances or granting leave; he had used oppressive discipline towards some, and favouritism towards others. It was alleged, for example, that a sergeant had been promoted to inspector and put in charge of the force's Traffic Branch even though he could not drive. It was also alleged that Wilcox was his nephew, and that his appointment had been decided upon before it was advertised.

Such charges, often little more than rumours, were easily dealt with. The accusation of a family relationship was disconcerting for Wilcox, not so much because it was easy to disprove, nor because Warren stressed that he had never set eyes on him before his selection interview, but because Warren went on to state, by way of emphasis, that Wilcox was not his first choice for the post. Wilcox appears to have been rather shaken by this comment and confessed to finding Warren always to be a little distant; nevertheless he began to grow fond of him, and when the opportunity to move on appeared after he had been in post for less than a year he sought Warren's advice and found him both helpful and encouraging.

The Move to Hertfordshire

Shortly after his return from Austria Nott-Bower moved up a rung at Scotland Yard; he was promoted from Assistant Commissioner to Deputy Commissioner. At the same time the Home Secretary, James Chuter Ede, and his advisors in the Home Office thought it time to bring some fresh blood into the senior ranks of the Metropolitan Police.

They offered Nott-Bower's old post to Arthur Young, who had been serving as Chief Constable of Hertfordshire for about two years. Young's move to London was highly unusual since provincial police officers had, as a rule, never been considered for such transfers and his appointment was not welcomed among the traditionalists in the Metropolitan Police. Not that this appears to have concerned Young very much, and probably not as much as finding himself tied to a desk. In Italy he had left day-to-day administration to Wilcox while he travelled inspecting his police and anything else that appeared relevant. He had a high opinion of Wilcox and, on his transfer to London, suggested that Wilcox apply for the Hertfordshire job. Wilcox had been in his new post in Buckinghamshire for about six months and believed that without Young's encouragement he would never have had the inclination to apply. It was at this point that he asked Warren's advice, as well as that of the chairman of the Standing Joint Committee. Since both were encouraging, he applied.

Now the bit was between Wilcox's teeth. He saw an advertisement requesting applications for the vacant post of Chief Constable of Devonshire. He knew Devonshire much better than Hertfordshire since it was close to his native Bristol and was more keen to get this appointment, so he fired off a second application. He was shortlisted for both posts and was called for interview in Hertford on 12 February 1947 and in Exeter on the following day; he was also slightly concerned about two others called for interview.

Among those on the Hertfordshire shortlist was Ranulph Bacon, an old colleague and friend from Hendon. 'Rasher' Bacon, as he was inevitably known, had a degree from Cambridge, had passed out of Hendon with the 'baton of honour', had been seconded from the Metropolitan Police during the war to serve as a Provost Marshal in North Africa and had then moved to Ceylon where, from 1944, he was Inspector General of Police.

'Rasher' was also on the Devonshire shortlist along with another Hendon friend, Herman Rutherford, who had shared the expensive experience of holidaying with Arthur Duveen, served with Wilcox in Italy and Austria, and was already Chief Constable of Oxfordshire.

Fortunately Wilcox did not have to be measured against Bacon for the Hertfordshire post, as the ship from Ceylon was late and he could not make the interview. Bacon's arrival made an impact in Exeter; John Skittery, another graduate of the first course at Hendon and now Chief Constable of Plymouth, met his ship and rushed him to the interviews that were already in progress. There appears to have been considerable excitement among the S.J.C. as to whether or not he would arrive, and whether or not he was the best choice – and Wilcox thought he was – the excitement gave an added lustre to his interview.

Rutherford, in contrast, found himself in the difficult position of having among his referees Lord Roche, the chair of the Oxfordshire Quarter Sessions and a Lord of Appeal in Ordinary, who had recently presented a Departmental Committee Report recommending that police officers should no longer present cases in magistrates' courts. Rutherford defended this recommendation before the interview board which, in contrast, was quite satisfied with the way that things were and had no desire to incur the expense of paying for solicitors for tasks that they felt their police were doing competently.

Wilcox doubted that he would ever have come out on top if Bacon had been able to make the Hertfordshire interview. He had little recollection of precisely how it had gone, though he did recall, after being told that the job was his subject to the Home Secretary's confirmation, being invited into the office of Bob Longmore, the Clerk of the County Council, who produced a bottle of whisky to celebrate the occasion. In consequence when the police doctor examined him immediately afterwards he expressed concern about Wilcox's pulse rate and requested a report from Wilcox's own doctor before certifying him as fit enough to take up the appointment.

He was fit enough for the post, but looking back on the development of the force he was slightly unnerved by the fact that the expectancy of time in the job for Chief Constables of Hertfordshire appeared to be getting shorter and shorter. The force had been established in 1841 and its first four chiefs had served for 39, 31, 17 and 11 years respectively.

Captain Sydney Fairman had taken over in 1939, but he had come from the Ministry of Transport and had little police experience. This was particularly unfortunate, as he followed a man who was feared and loathed by all ranks for the ways in which he set out to impress the S.J.C. by making cuts and saving money. Fairman resigned after three years and was followed by his long-suffering deputy, a decorated artilleryman of the First World War, but never made anything other than acting Chief Constable. He continued to serve in this role after Young's appointment until the latter was available to take over in April 1945; and he left after two years. 'At that rate of progression,' Wilcox mused, 'a statistician would give me no more than a year.'

During his two years leading the Hertfordshire force, Young had begun to reform and modernise it. He started to establish a fleet of motor vehicles, not least because the Great North Road, the A1, bisected his jurisdiction. He started the installation of a wireless system at the headquarters in Hatfield; and he began a programme of building police houses. The Chair of the County Finance Committee, on hearing of his appointment to Scotland Yard, is said to have expressed some relief with the words: 'We couldn't have afforded to keep him any longer.'

The county was rather busier than Buckinghamshire and was experiencing the beginning of major growth. It included old country towns as well as the City of St. Albans, with its Cathedral and, from the inter-war years, a growing electronics industry. The St. Albans City Police were amalgamated with Herts at the same time as Wilcox took command in the county.

Elsewhere in the county there were much newer cities. In the early years of the century Ebenezer Howard had established the first ever garden cities Letchworth in 1903 and Welwyn Garden City in 1920. In 1946, parliament passed the New Towns Act including provision for eight new towns around war-damaged London, three of which - Stevenage, Hatfield and Hemel Hempstead - were in Hertfordshire. Howard had envisaged his garden cities as being self-contained communities, but with their easy distance from London and decent road and railway links, Letchworth and Welwyn became like the other new towns, dormitories for large numbers who commuted to the capital. It was much the same with the more established town of Watford to the south-west of the county; its printing industry was soon to begin its decline, but it still had Scammell Lorries and, just outside the town, the de Havilland aircraft factory, both of which had boomed while equipping the army during the war, though their decline and closure was after Wilcox's time as Chief Constable.

Young's reforms had begun to establish and recruit a police body more aware of how things were changing. He had also succeeded in appointing two able assistants; Neil Galbraith came from the Lancashire Police to act as the chief clerk in the headquarters, and John Gott came from the Metropolitan Police to fill a Chief Inspector vacancy. Gott was another Hendon graduate, though he had attended the college three years after Wilcox; he had been decorated as a police inspector for his role in a rescue during the Blitz and then, on a second occasion, when a navigator in R.A.F. Bomber Command, for his courageous actions in dealing with an explosion and fire on his airfield. Gott was a motoring enthusiast who was killed at the wheel of a racing car. Both he and Galbraith served Wilcox well before Galbraith moved to be Chief Constable of Leicester City in

1956, Chief Constable of Monmouthshire later in the same year, and an Inspector of Constabulary in 1964. Gott became Chief Constable of Northamptonshire in 1960 until his death twelve years later.

Wilcox may have had able assistants and the beginnings of reform upon which he could build, but the county's S.J.C. appears to have been little changed since these bodies were first established in 1888. The Lord Lieutenant, Viscount Hampden, chaired the committee and had done so for the previous 27 years; he remained in the chair until 1952, when he had reached the age of 83 years. At Hampden's side was the 4th Marquess of Salisbury, the son of one of Queen Victoria's prime ministers; but he was only there for Wilcox's first meeting since he died, aged 85 years, shortly afterwards.

The 5th Marquess duly followed his father, though this was not for another 12 years, when the staunch conservative and ardent supporter of empire left his various political posts, including leader of the House of Lords, to grace the S.J.C. with his presence. It may be rather amusing and possibly shocking to see these elderly gentlemen as still listed as taking major roles in local government, yet in the immediate post-war world, their presence could be useful in what they brought to local issues. As peers of the realm and members of the House of Lords they could demand that Home Office ministers respond personally to their letters and that, if they insisted, the Home Secretary should receive them.

As elsewhere, since the legislation of 1888, half of the members of the S.J.C. were county magistrates and the other half were county councillors. Altogether, the Herts membership was around twenty. After the confrontational meeting that had been his first experience of such a committee in Buckinghamshire, Wilcox attended his first meeting with some trepidation. He need not have worried. Unlike his baptism of fire in Bucks, and unlike what he knew of the weekly meetings of the Watch Committee in Bristol, the quarterly gatherings in Herts were short and gentlemanly.

In Bristol, the Chief Constable had been required to give full details of crimes and events that had come to the attention of the police in the previous seven days. The quarterly S.J.C. meetings in

Herts wanted to see the crime statistics before they were passed to the county quarter sessions; they expected details on any matters of particular interest, and on any authority required for expenditure. It was not that the committee was idle and uninterested; indeed, at the first meeting Wilcox attended there was some discussion of the fact that a large proportion of detected offences had been committed by people under the age of 17 years. The Marquess of Salisbury agreed to tackle the Home Secretary about this, but since he died shortly after this no-one ever knew, or appeared to ask, whether there had been a meeting and, if so, what was the outcome. But generally there was little questioning of the Chief Constable at the meetings and little discussion or comment. Indeed, new members of the committee were expected not to say anything until they had served for a few years.

The upshot was that the S.J.C. meetings were generally completed after around 20 minutes and the members then spent roughly the same amount of time chatting with each other. They preferred to raise matters with the Chief Constable separately, in private and without making a fuss. Wilcox had no problem with this. After all, he reasoned, magistrates probably knew the local senior police officers better than the Chief Constable. Moreover, he believed, it was equally, if not more, important for the Chief Constable to be on good terms with the Clerk of the County Council. Wilcox had already found the Clerk, Bob Longmore, to be welcoming when he invited him into his office for a whisky on his appointment and they rapidly developed a good relationship, not the least recognising and respecting the boundaries of their different jurisdictions and responsibilities. On Longmore's retirement Wilcox built a similar relationship with his successor, Neville Moon.

Change Comes to the Beat

The decade or so after the Second World War has often been seen as a Golden Age for British policing. This was encapsulated in the 1950 feature film *The Blue Lamp*, which showed an idealised elderly constable, George Dixon, showing a new recruit the ropes. Dixon was shot dead in the film but was resurrected for a BBC series in 1955, which was to run for 21 years. He was a traditional, beat-pounding copper who knew his manor, its residents, and rarely had to confront murders or serious crimes. He began each television episode with a cheerful 'Evening all', and concluded the programme with a short homily about the story that they had just seen.

Yet the period of Dixon's popularity coincided with considerable change. Some academics have written of the 'desacralization' of the police during the period, driven by inexorably rising crime statistics and a decline in police/public relations, especially as more of the population became car owners and drivers and therefore subject, for the first time, to police-enforced regulations. Whether or not the desacralization thesis is valid, it is also the case that the police themselves also had a number of problems in the job during these years – they were understrength, pay was poor and there were limited opportunities.

In his unpublished memoir, Wilcox suggested that there were 'three essentials in running a police force... first, recruiting the right kind of men and women; next, giving them the right kind of training; and then promoting the right kind of officers.' When he assumed command in Herts there were problems in all of these areas. The war had a major impact on the numbers of regular police; potential young recruits had been sent into the armed services, old men expecting to retire had been kept on, and the ranks had been filled with various auxiliaries, notably part-time special constables. Training remained rooted in a particular understanding of nineteenth-century society and its requirements; and in many respects this understanding had been as irrelevant for much of Victoria's England as it was to the one that followed the Second World War. Promotion often still had elements of Buggins' turn; and this was aggravated in the eyes of some of the men who came home from the war having achieved a significant military rank, who were expected to return to their old police pre-war rank and who found that some of those that had stayed at home had been promoted above them. These promoted men were usually entitled to wear, as one R.A.F. veteran put it, only 'a very lonely Defence Medal ribbon (a gong given to Boy Scouts).'

The Herts Police establishment of 613 had 156 vacancies when Wilcox took command. It is interesting to find him writing about recruiting men and women as many Chief Constables were hostile to the idea of women officers, only accepting them as a wartime necessity and using them to make tea and do the typing. For a generation after the war, most women officers were restricted to a female sphere, dealing almost entirely with women and children. This is not to say that Wilcox was an ardent supporter of women covering every area of policing, he remained a man of his time; but he was not one of the crusty dinosaurs who considered that if they had to be appointed, then women officers should be kept doing 'women's' work – making tea, typing and dealing with women and children.

The traditional view was that the prevention of crime was the principal task of the police, and that this was best achieved by beat patrols made on foot. The idea had appeared at the beginning of the Instructions prepared for the first Metropolitan Police officers when they took to the streets of London in September 1829, and since then it had become the keystone of policing for senior police officers and politicians, and passed on down to the men on the beat whose task it was to walk at a steady two-and-a-half miles an hour.

In 1954, in his book *Scotland Yard*, Sir Harold Scott, who had just retired as Commissioner of the Metropolitan Police, declared:

> The is no real substitute ... for the man on the beat or patrol who, as he goes round his area, gets to know the people and the buildings and is quick to notice any unusual circumstances that may turn out to be significant.

In many respects, he may have been right. Yet while a constable might easily patrol one of the tightly-defined beats of central London or any other big city, and might easily summon assistance by, in the early years, springing his rattle and later by blowing his whistle, on their fringes such cities had open country districts where the close deployment of men was impracticable. In rural districts and for the police in rural counties it was the same. Here, the distances covered by patrolling officers were much greater, often lonely and could rarely be done regularly every day. Moreover, the distances between police houses, where a man lived with his wife and family, could be considerable.

Like others of his more forceful and outspoken colleagues, Wilcox raised hackles when, recognising the problem of constables spread thinly across the county in a rapidly changing world, he proposed to transfer to expanding towns the number of police officers living in villages with no more than around 100 to 200 inhabitants. A good fleet of police motor vehicles meant that such areas could be policed much more easily and quickly than by a man on foot or a push-bike; and such police cars were necessary anyway, because of the growth of motor ownership among the general population and the fact that Herts was bisected by the major north-south trunk road, the A1. Even so, parish councils and the local squirearchy were particularly unhappy about the loss of their village police officer.

Other plans for reorganising the divisional structure so that it was more in line with the way in which the county's population was changing and developing were even more unpopular. Many magistrates appear particularly to have resented the fact that this would replace the superintendents, who they liked to see in their courts, with inspectors of what were in future to be divisional sub-divisions.

Yet given population growth and the percentage shift in location, it was much more sensible to have divisional headquarters in the county town of Hertford, rather than in Bishop's Stortford, in Welwyn rather than Hatfield, and in Stevenage rather than Hitchin.

Other changes were not as unpopular; they fostered the belief that the police were at the forefront of modernisation to engage with a changing world. The problem was the expense, though not when the Home Office could be seen to take much of the strain.

Wilcox had observed two-way radio contact between a station and police patrol cars during his visit to the United States in the mid-1930s. The Metropolitan Police were experimenting with wireless communications before the war, but the general belief was that

Morse Code was better than speech as it was possible that anyone outside the police who was in possession of a transmitter and so inclined could pick up what was being said; and Wilcox had been assured before he left for America that it was not possible to use radios in cities because of other forms of interference. One of the things that he had pointed out in the report which he wrote on his return was the clarity available on American police radios in spite of steel-ribbed skyscrapers and electrified elevated railways. Some British provincial Chief Constables had begun successful experiments with wireless systems during the inter-war period; but this unfortunately left a legacy of different, sometimes incompatible frequencies between neighbouring forces.

As noted earlier, Wilcox replaced Arthur Young in Herts shortly before the wireless system that Young had initiated, with Home Office backing, was up and running. He had scarcely a month to familiarise himself with it before, on 2 June 1947 Chuter Ede came to Hatfield to inaugurate what Wilcox called the first stage of the national police wireless network. With the usual political spin on the superiority of the police in Britain, Chuter Ede announced it as the first of its kind in the world; and perhaps Wilcox was slightly over-egging the pudding with reference to his own force's role. There were, as he admitted, extensive teething troubles. It took a decade to iron out the incompatibilities between different systems and local forces continued to conduct their own, significant, experiments.

The new technology available to the police led to a further rethinking of the beat patrol. In Aberdeen, the Chief Constable launched an experiment with sergeants and six constables being deployed from their station in a police van and dropped off for short spells in different parts of the city. This meant that potential offenders could never be sure where a beat patrol might be. The system was copied across the United Kingdom by different Chief Constables in some of the towns within their jurisdiction. Wilcox tried it in Watford, but he reported that it was unpopular with constables, who preferred to take responsibility for their own individual beats. This may, of course, have been little more than a reluctance to change from what serving officers knew and understood; the individual beat was traditional practice. Wilcox decided to revert back to the old practice.

A few years later a variant of the Aberdeen system was established in some Lancashire towns, most notably Kirby, a new town on the Lancashire edge of the city of Liverpool. The town planners had built houses, but they had largely ignored the provision of shops and social amenities; Kirby developed an unenviable reputation for crime and violence, and insufficient police. Under the Chief Constable, Eric St. Johnston, what was to become known as Unit Beat Policing was launched using some Aberdonian features. A resident beat constable in a police car and equipped with a pocket radio could report in, summon assistance and pass on any information that might usefully be collated and noted at the local station.

The Home Office liked the scheme, it seemed like a way of saving manpower so it offered money for the purpose of purchasing cars and radio equipment. The money had to be spent within a financial year, and while several Chief Constables were sceptical about whether the Unit Beat System was relevant for their force, they were happy to persuade their police committees that they should accept the offer of cars and radios which they wanted, though they also retained the right to use these as they saw fit.

The Chief Constable of West Sussex, Ronald Wilson, was one of those who liked the Unit Beat Policing idea, and developed it for the new town of Crawley. He put a constable into each of the neighbourhoods that had been established by the planners of Crawley; the man had 24-hour responsibility for his patch, but could use discretion over his hours on duty. Wilcox sent a superintendent to study Wilson's system. He came back full of enthusiasm, and under Wilcox's gaze a similar plan was prepared for the policing of Hatfield, Hemel Hempstead, Stevenage and Welwyn Garden City. Hemel Hempstead was the first Herts town to have the system up and running, in February 1962.

In addition to the new towns, the growth of motor traffic necessitated changes to the old style of beat policing, particularly on major roads. Herts had a number of roads running into London and to its docks, which meant heavy lorries passing through, often parking overnight in lay-bys or in the car parks of cafes. The valuable cargoes on these lorries made them targets for thefts and hijackings. The problem led Wilcox to establish joint meetings at Hatfield with senior C.I.D. officers from the Metropolitan Police to co-ordinate plans to deal with the situation. In return, the Commissioner invited Wilcox to send his own detectives on attachment to Scotland Yard and a group emerged popularly known as the Home and Colonial Squad.

But while some lorry thefts might have been prevented or quickly solved as a result of the exchanges, and while co-operation between the Metropolitan Police and the Herts Police led to the arrest of Harry Roberts who had shot dead three London constables in August 1966, nothing prevented the steady growth of crime during the 1950s and 1960s. This was a malaise that affected the entire western world and not something confined to Herts. Wilcox was aware of this overall growth, yet it did not stop his frustration and his determination to recruit and keep the best men and women possible for his force.

Recruiting, Training, Promotion

The Hertfordshire Police were a medium-sized county force; it was marginally larger than that of Buckinghamshire, but in the same sort of mould. The reduction in police numbers that followed the onset of peace across the whole country meant the need for a recruiting programme. It took three years for Herts to get its pre-war authorised establishment restored, and Wilcox was worried that his force was slipping behind in the amount of cover that it could provide. He believed that the incessant demands from some sections of the public for more and more police had to be resisted, since uniformed officers on every street corner and the constant ringing of police car bells, and later shrieking two-note sirens, implied an oppressive police presence. He was enough of a man brought up at the beginning of the twentieth century to believe in much of the traditional image of the British Bobby. 'We prefer an unobtrusive police service,' he wrote in his memoir, 'available when needed.' Even so, he was soon convinced that he needed more officers.

Not long after the force reached its pre-war authorised establishment of 613, Wilcox estimated that he needed an increase to 820 so as to deal with the emerging changes in Hertfordshire. Gordon Halland, who had returned to the Inspectorate of Constabulary in 1947, supported him; but looking at the costs the Standing Joint Committee was alarmed, and sent a deputation to the Home Office which proposed a reduction in numbers. Unfortunately for the deputation, it had to deal with the tough, no nonsense Permanent Under Secretary, Sir Frank Newsam, whose only concession was to allow the increase to be made in two stages.

Wilcox continued to review the size of the force until his retirement, by which time its authorised strength had doubled from the time that he took over, but there were 300 vacancies.

For a generation after the war, pay was a key problem in police recruitment. During the inter-war years the maximum of a constable's pay was slightly more than half that of an ordinary industrial worker. In addition, the police officer enjoyed various perks such as accommodation, or money in lieu, paid holidays, a pension and immunity from unemployment. Wartime saw the erosion of this position; even with wartime supplements, the pay of those at work in industry began to catch up and overtake the pay of police officers. Police perks remained, but full employment after the war further undermined the position of a police officer's pay, and this was in spite of a series of investigations beginning in 1948 with the committee chaired by Lord Oaksey. This committee was charged with considering the best way to recruit and retain suitable men and women, investigating specifically promotion, pensions, pay and allowances. Like its successors, the Oaksey committee recommended a pay increase; unfortunately rising industrial pay rates rapidly wiped out each increase almost as soon as it was agreed. Neither Wilcox nor any other Chief Constable could do much about nationally-determined wage rates, and even if they could, the Standing Joint Committees and Watch Committees probably would have been very reluctant to find the additional money.

Another national regulation introduced by the Home Office irritated Wilcox. In an effort to encourage more men to apply for the police, the minimum height was reduced for recruits to five feet nine inches. Wilcox himself was well over six feet. He looked back nostalgically to the old Bristol City Force, which when he joined insisted that its men be at least five feet eleven inches. Others had insisted that men be at least six feet. When it was pointed out to Wilcox that some of Britain's finest military commanders would never have been accepted into a police force under the old height regulations, his response was that soldiers were not policemen. The former were expected to be aggressive, the latter had to exercise restraint. People seemed to put greater confidence in big men. Moreover, height made a man more visible which, he believed, probably contributed to better behaviour on the policeman's part.

Wilcox also lamented that while many of the young men applying to take the police entrance test had sufficient basic general knowledge to pass, as well as sufficient ability in reading, writing and doing simple arithmetic, it was depressing to read their sloppy English. He complained to the Director of Education in Herts, who urged him to visit a local teacher training centre. He took with him some of those essays that were, in his opinion, the worst. He was met with the response that insistence on grammar and spelling only served to stifle creativity. If the meaning could be deciphered then there was no problem. Wilcox was not happy; he pointed out that the entries in police notebooks 'were examined by solicitors, counsel and judges. They would have little confidence in the reliability of the police if their reports were full of misspellings and grammatical errors.' He could do nothing about wage rates and height reductions but, reluctant to turn away potentially competent young recruits, he could work on their use of the English language during their training.

Local police forces had to send their recruits to one of eight district training centres immediately after the war. Herts recruits went to Eynsham Hall, a manor house near Witney in Oxfordshire; and the development of the syllabus proceeded as a snail's pace with the concentration on legal definitions remaining central. Wilcox believed that such training was not very exciting, and of little use to the inexperienced constable nervously patrolling his first beat. He thought that possibly it left the constable confused and inhibited from using plain common-sense; though he would never have gone as far as many of the old sweat sergeants, who told young constables to forget everything that the training school had tried to teach them. In contrast to educationalists who wanted the period of training extended over several years, Wilcox wanted a mix of three months intensive instruction, though without the lawyer-like approach to the law, followed by a period of practical experience and then refresher courses.

Giving evidence in court was an experience as nerve-wracking for the young constable as walking the beat alone for the first time; the young constable knew what he was supposed to do but, again, it was experience and practice that helped. When Wilcox joined the Bristol City Police in the late 1920s, it was the practice that constables paraded before the superintendent an hour before the magistrates' court began its sitting and recited their evidence to him. The superintendent then sat in the court to listen and watch; but in general the entire proceedings did not last more than a couple of hours.

Like many other things, the situation was changing after the Second World War. Counties still had three different kinds of court within their boundaries: in the magistrates' courts three local worthies, appointed as magistrates, adjudicated on minor offences; the quarter sessions met four times a year and here, amongst other things, magistrates in much larger numbers and chaired by an experienced barrister heard more serious cases, though the verdict was left to a jury; assize courts were presided over by judges from outside the county and, again, juries decided the verdict on the evidence presented.

Wilcox found that he was expected to be present at both quarter sessions and assizes, though he was unsure where and how the authority for his appearance at the former had emerged. For several years, when the quarter sessions opened, he sat in for a couple of hours; he also attended if he noted that a particularly interesting case was to be heard. Yet increasingly he preferred to get on with other things and entrusted his detective superintendent to attend and watch over matters. The detective superintendent was also a much better choice, since Wilcox and the Clerk of the Peace agreed to let the superintendent relieve the clerk from the task of distributing briefs for the prosecution. Such distribution still needed to be fair, but the superintendent acquired knowledge of the performance of different counsel.

On Wilcox's arrival in Herts the police were required to provide a staff of ushers for the quarter sessions. He did not think that this was a particularly useful way to deploy police officers and urged the use of civilian ushers, who might be identified by gowns, to take over the job. He appointed 15 men and women for the position and it was rapidly extended to the magistrates' courts. However, the proposal to have such ushers for the assizes ran into problems. The assizes in Herts were already becoming relatively low key affairs; there were no mounted police to escort the judge and no javelin men to march at his side, though a welcoming fanfare of trumpets survived. The judges objected that civilian ushers would deprive their court of police protection; but perhaps more seriously, the Treasury objected to the scale of the ushers' fees.

The Treasury eventually agreed to the scheme to be tried on an experimental basis, but then appeared to have forgotten about it. There was no enquiry as to how it was working so, in the silence, Wilcox carried on. County money was saved in other ways, notably the reduction of the entertainment that accompanied the assizes. There was a tradition that the judge retired to his own room for lunch at mid-day. The Herts County Sheriff, however, lavishly entertained senior counsel and his guests. The guests, who included the Chief Constable, were not required to return to the court when the judge commenced the afternoon session, and Wilcox admitted to enjoying the wine and coffee that continued to flow. Then, in 1952, Sir David Bowes-Lyon, the younger brother of the recently widowed Queen, became High Sheriff and established much plainer lunches. Wilcox could see that this was much more in keeping with the business of trying serious cases in the adjacent court room where the judge sat in his wig and red robes, and where his nervous young constables gave their evidence and faced questions from bewigged, black-gowned counsel.

Constables could not be recruited and sworn in until they had reached the age of 19. Wilcox, like others, believed that this was cutting off a significant number of competent youngsters that left school at 15 who, by the time that they had reached the age when they could join the police, had already found a trade or a job offering a decent career. During the nineteenth-century it had been the practice among some of the larger forces to recruit young men to work as clerks; if they proved themselves competent they could expect to follow a fast track to sergeant. Wilcox himself had been recruited in Bristol while technically under age, though he had seen no opportunity for any sort of promotion. When Arthur Young moved to Hertfordshire he had recruited some boy clerks and posted them to divisional stations; the divisions, however, appear to have had little idea of what to do with them and they were used to run errands and make tea.

Wilcox decided to improve on this. The second report of Lord Oaksey's committee which included a discussion of the education problem was published in November 1949. Within a year, Wilcox had established 'cadets' for his force; He brought the boys to his headquarters, put them into uniform, and arranged for the local education authority to bring in tutors so as to improve their education.

The cadet scheme was underway by 1949, though there were to be no female cadets for another seventeen years. Much to Wilcox's disappointment, initially it was impossible to provide the male cadets with residential accommodation, but they were able to have two weeks in a Victorian mansion and, as a toughening up exercise, they spent another two weeks in Snowdonia climbing the hills, bathing in bitterly cold rivers and taking part in mountain rescue training. Wilcox and Ethel made a point of visiting each of these annual expeditions to Snowdonia; Ethel always provided a large cake to be enjoyed at the end of the trip, and on one occasion put it on the back seat of their car on a warm day when the sun shone and melted the icing on top. She saved the situation by coming to an arrangement with the chef at their hotel that she should provide a new cake and that he could have everything that she had left over.

Back in Herts the cadets were attached to hospitals, homes for the elderly and for those labelled in the parlance of the time as 'handicapped.' Much of this was done with the help of Alec Dickson, who founded Voluntary Service Overseas in 1958; and in 1963 one of Wilcox's cadets was sent to Pakistan on a V.S.O. trip. Wilcox also arranged for his cadets to visit centres of police technology, in other words the radio information room and the photographic department. They had a trip in a patrol car and visited the magistrates' court. Police courses for boys were established at the Haileybury and Imperial Service College. Wilcox was keen to see how his cadets measured up against the public school boys at the college. When the cadets reached the age of 19 they were sent with other recruits to Eynsham Hall, but they had a head start over other recruits, many of whom were in their mid-20s.

Wilcox was keen to ensure that his officers had opportunities and that, while the pay may never have been particularly high, they were keen to stay on either as ordinary patrolling constables or, for a period at least, trying out some other aspect of police work. Unlike the Metropolitan Police, Wilcox was not prepared to let the Herts C.I.D. become a force within a force whose members considered themselves to be possessed of unique expertise and superior intelligence. This separation, he believed, was not good for force cohesion; moreover, it could lead detectives to become a little too close to some of the dubious individuals that they were supposed to keep an eye on. In Wilcox's force, if a detective was promoted he could find himself filling a vacancy back in uniform.

When the first section of Britain's first motorway, the M1, was formally opened in November 1959 it passed through four police jurisdictions. There was talk of forming a traffic unit under a single command. Wilcox vigorously resisted the proposal. Motorway patrols offered another new opportunity for his men. He was worried that it could be a first step towards a national police system. In addition, he insisted that he had seen new organisations established abroad which had achieved little other than creating duplication and considerable expense, but which had not resulted in any improved efficiency. Wilcox won the argument; he also seized the opportunity to provide training for the traffic patrols of the four forces that were affected by the motorway.

Wilcox was always concerned about the police becoming nationalised and therefore, should there be any significant change in the political system, he worried that the police might become what he saw as a political tool. Nevertheless Chief Constables, their S.J.C.s or watch committees were never entirely free agents in respect of capital expenditure and schemes were commonly controlled and prioritised by the Home Office. Wilcox always had his own priorities about police developments and, particularly, how best to provide for his subordinates. As far as possible he sought to ensure that they came first in matters of well-being and opportunities at work and in their private life.

When he was interviewed for the position in Herts, the County Hall was a new building opened on the eve of the war; the Police headquarters, in contrast, consisted of a cottage built in 1883, a couple of Nissen huts, and a disused aircraft hanger which housed the traffic fleet. The police stations were in equally poor condition and inadequate. Wilcox thought that it would not look good if the headquarters was prioritised over the buildings from which most of his officers had to work and to welcome members of the public who were sometimes very distressed. Fifteen new divisional and sub-divisional police stations were completed during his time in office.

As the new police stations appeared, so did new accommodation for police officers and their families. Arthur Young had also seen the value of good accommodation to attract recruits and keep good officers. Wilcox did the same, and 826 houses were built during his time as Chief Constable; the old village houses were turned into places where interviews might be conducted and reports stored.

In Buckinghamshire he had arranged for police wives to speak with the architect responsible for building police houses; in Herts he arranged for a committee of constables and their wives similarly to meet with the county architect. The new houses were sited mainly in the expanding and new towns. The S.J.C. was perfectly happy to see bathrooms included in the plans, but there were some elderly members who could not understand that a police officer might have a family car and that a garage or space for parking was therefore desirable. Wilcox won them over apparently by arguing that it would be difficult for a police officer to enforce regulations against obstruction if he was known always to leave his own car parked in the street. In 1955 he authorised a scheme whereby men could decorate police houses themselves; the police authority supplied materials but, on satisfactory conclusion of the work, the police officer received £2 as a reward and to cover the cost of brushes, filler and paste. This scheme, known as 'Help Yourself', appears to have been popular, not least with those responsible for organising the police finances, who found the scheme much cheaper than the old practice of paying outside decorators and tradesmen. During the 1960s, however, in addition to buying their own cars, more and more police officers began buying their own houses. The police officer always received a tax-free allowance in lieu of not living in police accommodation; and the county council was not displeased because empty police houses could be offered to other employees such as those working in local government or as teachers.

The new headquarters was not opened until the year before Wilcox retired, and while putting this at the bottom of his building list he was determined that it should be state-of-the-art for police management and direction, and that it should provide good opportunities for rest and recreation for those in the job. It had been the practice in many county forces to settle their headquarters into large country houses. Herts itself was offered the estate of Lord Desborough, whose committee in the aftermath of the First World War had been instrumental in establishing a degree of uniformity and initiating at least a degree of change. Unfortunately, the county architect's assessment was that the accompanying house was beyond renovation.

The situation was solved by the Welwyn Garden City Development Corporation, which offered a 30 acre site, formerly a rubbish tip. This suited Wilcox perfectly since it kept him and his force at what he felt to be sufficient arm's length from County Hall in Hertford. Equally, it helped to scupper a proposal for a combined headquarters for the County Police and the County Fire Brigade. Stirred, perhaps, by his remembrance of the representatives of the British Fire Brigades Union at the conference which he had attended in Paris, Wilcox wrote in his memoir that he was determined to ensure that the maintenance of his police vehicles was never 'in the hands of mechanics who were members of the Fire Brigade Union affiliated to the T.U.C.'

When it opened, Wilcox's headquarters had everything that was deemed necessary for a modern police force of the time: the necessary offices, a canteen and a dining room; a communications block with a radio mast; garages, workshops and a skid pan for the traffic unit; classrooms for training and hostels for the cadets and visitors.

Wilcox was determined that it should also provide his officers with opportunities for recreation and fitness; as a consequence, there were playing fields, a gymnasium and a swimming pool that could be used in all weathers, night and day. The latter created problems. The Home Office raised a series of objections and stated its preference for a bowling green. With some prompting from Wilcox, it seems, the Herts authorities resolved on a deputation to expedite matters, and the Home Office appears to have been a little surprised by the august figures that lined up to attend: the chair of the S.J.C., the Lord Lieutenant, Lord Salisbury and the clerk to the county council. The

Permanent Under Secretary deputed to face this formidable group of Hertfordshire's great and good promised that the Home Secretary would give their request 'sympathetic consideration', and approval for the pool arrived a month later.

Recruiting and bringing on potentially bright young people to fill the ranks was one thing; providing them with a good working environment and decent housing perks was another. But Wilcox also wanted to ensure that the best of them made it into leadership roles, and that the notion of Buggins' turn was no longer one of the guiding principles for promotion. The Oaksey committee had recommended selection boards for promotions and, once again, Wilcox was quick off the mark and had them up and running by 1950. Yet in his memoir, he confessed that he was not a great fan of such boards. He felt that they tended to favour the person who could think quickly and produce a slick answer. But until someone thought of something better, the selection board appeared the best way to suggest that there was fairness in the system. Wilcox sought to emphasise this by beginning a board with a resumé of the candidate's career which, if nothing else, proved that his or her file had been read; moreover, he believed that these introductory moments gave the candidate a bit of time to get their breath and relax into the proceedings. He instructed the superintendents on the board not to ask questions about police duties; after all, the candidate had already sat and passed a promotion exam. Unfortunately, he recalled, this tended to make the interview concentrate on asking candidates about the games and sports that they played, and the books and newspapers that they read; it was surprising, he remembered, how many of them spoke of reading *The Times*. In the end, the board rarely departed from the recommendation of the candidate's superior, even though it was aware that the current post might have brought the candidate to the limit of his or her abilities.

Overall, Wilcox appears to have kept morale reasonably high in the Herts police through his encouragements of cadets, his determination to give his officers up-to-date working conditions, opportunities for rest and relaxation and decent housing.

Other reforms kept abreast of social change that led to new problems for his officers. In 1965, for example, partly in response to what looked to be a rise in violent confrontations between youth gangs, he created a Tactical Patrol Group of an inspector, a sergeant and ten constables, whose task it was to deal with serious public order problems.

During that same year there were 26 prosecutions for illegal possession of drugs and the numbers appeared to be rising, in response to which he established a drug squad of three, a detective sergeant and two detective constables (one male and one female), at the beginning of 1967. In its first year, the new squad dealt with two deaths from drug overdoses and made 89 arrests.

Though many were opposed, he managed to introduce more civilian workers into the force, which freed officers for more specific police tasks; thus, a police matron was appointed to Watford Station in 1964 to relieve female officers of the need to attend female prisoners. Three years later he had nine civilian garage mechanics, 18 driver-cleaners and 150 administrative and clerical workers. The 99 traffic wardens also counted as civilian staff. Opponents of these measures protested that civilians might give away confidential police information. Wilcox manifestly had little time for such arguments; moreover, by appointing many ex-police officers to these posts, he was able to draw the sting of the objections.

His experiments with communications were more mixed. The Police Pillar system had been established in the independent city force of St. Albans during the 1930s. As elsewhere, it was found that the patrolling constable used the telephone in the box regularly as expected, but the general public appeared reluctant to use the police phone to report anything untoward. St. Albans City Police were amalgamated with Hertfordshire in 1947, and Wilcox determined to spread the pillar system into the county, though with no more success in encouraging the public to use the phones. The situation was improved, at least on the police side, but not until almost 18 years later when the first pocket radios were supplied to beat officers in Stevenage; and in the following year, 1966, a smaller UHF phone rather than the original VHF one was introduced.

The least successful of his reforms, however - police aircraft that could be used in searches and for taking photographs - folded in 1960 after some four years, with no alternative replacement. The Police Flying Club was technically a private organisation, though to be a member it was necessary to belong to the Herts Police. The pilots appear almost entirely to have been wartime pilots who had gone on to acquire a civilian licence; they had also acquired an old Tiger Moth as the club's plane. They promised to provide the plane, with a trained crew, at the disposal of the police authority for any purpose for which it might prove fit. The problem was that flying was an expensive hobby. The trained pilots moved away, and there was no provision for training replacements or making significant contributions to the club from the finances available to the Herts police.

◆

Wilcox retired as Chief Constable of Hertfordshire in 1969. He received a glowing tribute for his achievements in the Annual Report presented by Raymond Buxton, his successor. Leaders generally receive glowing accounts of their service when they retire, yet these seem genuine and the members of the force appear to have held him in high regard.

But what such accounts do is focus on service within an institution. What are equally important in Wilcox's case are his more general activities to the police service and to the criminal justice system over the years while he was in Hertfordshire and after he retired. It also shrouds his home life and his staunch commitment to his family.

CHAPTER 7

HOME AND AWAY

The Family Man

At the end of January 1946 Wilcox replied to a letter that he had just received from Ethel. He had just returned to Vienna, and in her letter she had described two recent radio programmes called 'What does separation do to you?'

'As I haven't heard them,' he replied,

> I shall be able to go on in blissful ignorance of my mistakes. I'm convinced now that my policy of treating a month's leave as a period of rest is quite wrong. But here we are on the go all the time ... A month's idleness is too great a reaction. When I was home I must say I wasn't feeling very fit, but here I'm all right again, at least that's what I think.

Within a year, however, the pressure of Public Safety in Vienna was exchanged for a job at home and life with his family. Like many young fathers in the first half of the 1940s, Wilcox had rarely been around to see his two daughters in their early years. Indeed, however much Ethel told them of their father, Susan and Bridget must have found it a surprise when this big man moved in with them and stayed.

While he was away, Wilcox found a postcard with a long trail of children spread across it. He sent it to Ethel, writing on the back: 'The picture of our family to be.' Stephen was born at the end of 1948, but there the Wilcox trail was to end.

Hertfordshire provided the new Chief Constable and his family with a large house. There was an extensive garden with a tree house and a pond. The children loved it; and of course a very small Stephen fell in the pond. The garden suited animals. Susan acquired a goat, and there were an assortment of cats, geese and dogs. One of the latter came from the police; it had been rejected as too soft for a police dog. Everyone assumed that she had been spayed, until she produced eight puppies.

Wilcox read to the children when they went to bed and he began to write stories for them. When she was seven, Susan was diagnosed with polio in her left foot and lower leg and she spent a considerable time in hospital, and Wilcox wrote her a story. Called 'Hidden in Herts' it was centred around Hertfordshire landmarks and a pack of playing cards, and concerned a family called Elliott closely resembling the Wilcoxes, with two small girls called Sally and Belinda. Wilcox wrote a chapter a day, and Ethel remembered bringing them on the visits that she was allowed. She thought that, once the story became known, the nurses were as keen to read the next instalment as Susan.

There were no stories when Stephen went to Haileybury College, but there were regular letters, invariably quite humorous. On one occasion, Stephen returned to school with a collection of very hard apples and instead of eating them they were used as missiles in the dormitory. 'When you are filling in your leisure time at school windows,' his father suggested, 'why choose to throw stones or golf balls or apples? Lightly poached eggs thrown at a window make quite a satisfactory mess without breaking the glass. You could get a dozen eggs (small size) for about 3/6d.'

The nature of Wilcox's job meant that he had many visitors, and there were also visits from old wartime friends who, like him, were still serving in the police. Visiting day was commonly Sunday, and Ethel remembered herself 'slogging' in the kitchen regularly.

There were occasional visits to the homes of local worthies such as Sir David Bowes-Lyon, and gatherings with the latter might also mean rubbing shoulders with the Queen Mother. Neither Wilcox nor his wife were great fans of cocktail parties; Ethel always claimed that she could not dance, but cocktails and balls went with the job. Lunches and dinners were easier, and Wilcox was often asked to speak about his war experience – particularly his opinion on the police of other European states – and about the police in general. He also took the opportunity of speaking on such subjects to schools, and from the surviving drafts of talks that he gave to Sixth forms he presented some serious information in a relatively light-hearted fashion and spent much of his time telling them a recent ripping yarn from the Herts force. In 1953, for example, he returned to an issue that he had addressed before the war in the *Police Journal*, pointing out that fictional detectives broke the law with impunity, issuing threats, laying traps and breaking into property. Real policing was much more boring and while an officer might, occasionally, run into excitement...

> he does not spend all his mornings interrogating the guests of a country house with the body lying in the library, or his afternoons pursuing crooks across the country in a high powered car, or his evenings in exclusive night clubs supplying beautiful girls with champagne.

But from here he went on to describe a recent case involving the arrest and conviction of a burglar who had been active in Harpenden, St. Albans and Watford. The man had been caught by careful, if uninteresting, police observation in Herts and liaison with the Metropolitan Police who watched antique dealers where the offender was believed to be selling his loot. From now on, the man's name, photograph and *modus operandi* would be on police records.

Two years later, in 1955, he spoke to the boys at Haileybury and began by promising to limit the educational bit of his talk on the basic principles that governed the police to ten minutes, and after that he discussed the problem of lorry theft on the roads to and from London. He illustrated this section with the story of the theft of a lorry carrying 15 tons of copper wire. The theft had been committed by a small gang organised by a London builder who appears to have intended to profit by using the wire in his building ventures.

His humour and one or two suggestions in his talks did not always go down well with some special interest groups. In particular, he upset motorcycle enthusiasts and salesmen by suggesting that motorcycles were dangerous. He did this particularly when he suggested to schoolgirls that it was inadvisable to ride pillion, and that they should find a boyfriend who had a car. When he spoke at his daughters' school towards the end of 1960 – a 'terrifying experience', speaking at a girls' school, he told his audience at the outset – he urged the girls to wait driving home with their boyfriend until he had a car, and he expressed his pleasure in hearing that the Sixth formers at the school were being given driving lessons of their own. 'Speaking as the father of two daughters, one of 19 and the other 17,' he went on,

> one of the horrors of the Christmas holidays for fathers is having to drive a daughter to a party or dance at 8 o'clock in the evening and then having to turn out again after midnight to fetch her back. There is always that dreadful quarter of an hour trying to make conversation with other gloomy fathers while the young people are finishing the last dance and putting on their coats. No wonder the constant cry of fathers to their daughters is: "Why can't you find a young man with a car to take you to parties?"

A similar statement made six months later, when he opened a footbridge over a road that cut a school from its playing fields, had a much larger, public audience and incensed the motorcycle community. The comments were reported in the local press, which wrote of a light-hearted affair, addressed by Wilcox with a few words that made the girls laugh. Yet the General Secretary of the Mid-Herts Motor Cycle and Car Club did not read the report in this way and pointed out that the police drove fast motorcycles on the M1. *Motor Cycling and Scooter Weekly* made a similar point; and the Federation of National and One-Make Motor Cycle Clubs wrote to him suggesting that it would have been more sensible on his part to have urged the girls to make sure that their boyfriends received proper instruction when they bought their first motorbike.

Perhaps Wilcox lamented his comments and the attempts to raise a smile. He does not appear to have raised any objection to two wheels propelled by an engine when, during the early 1950s, Ethel had acquired an Italian motor scooter. She would drive to the local shops with Stephen riding behind her, his back against hers so that he could wave to the traffic. Neither had a crash helmet; Ethel simply held her hair in place with a head scarf. She was well-known in the community for driving in this fashion, which says much about traffic conditions and regulation in the period. In many ways this undermined his warning about riding pillion on motorcycles, but none of his critics brought the matter up and were probably ignorant of it. As far as Ethel was concerned, after a few years she exchanged the scooter for a bubble car and Stephen acquired a number of friends who thought it much more fun to leave school in the bubble car rather than in their parents' saloons.

The scooter, and then the bubble car, may have led Ethel to appear a little eccentric to some. At the same time, out of uniform, Wilcox himself began to focus on his image as an English gentleman. When the family went on a skiing holiday in Switzerland he insisted that he would wear a suit which, naturally, was totally impractical. Ethel recalled that he could be very stubborn; but when she and Susan got him a rather more appropriate outfit for skiing, he appears rapidly to have yielded his obstinacy. Moreover, for all that he cultivated his English gentleman's image, both Wilcox and Ethel were determined that their children should grow up with a good grasp of foreign cultures and languages. They travelled abroad on family holidays, but the children also travelled to stay with Ethel's Swiss relations and with Max Pammer's family.

As the family grew up the holidays became increasingly separate. Wilcox drove Ethel down the route that he had taken with Duveen about thirty years earlier. He also drove her to Salerno. On each occasion he found it difficult to recognise places at they had been; trees, for example, had grown up in much of the area that he had liberated to make it unrecognisable from what he remembered in September and October 1943. He vowed never again to make return journeys of this sort. Ethel wrote letters telling the children about where they had been and what they had seen. Wilcox described the food and drink.

But parents and children still made occasional trips together. In 1964, the year after she graduated, Susan organised to travel to India by bus. Ethel was reluctant to have her travelling to countries that she herself had not seen and flew out to meet her in the Lebanon. Susan's links with India grew; she worked there for Air France and became deeply involved with a small charity working with street children. When she urged her parents to visit, Wilcox suggested that he meet her halfway – somewhere like Dover, he jokingly suggested. Bridget remembered similar teasing. Whenever she visited her parents from her home in Edinburgh, among his first words were: 'When are you going back?'

Official Visits and Official Committees

At one point during 1965 Wilcox sat down to work out how many days he had spent away from the Herts Police in a month. It worked out as 13, during which time he had attended meetings at the Home Office and the Ministry of Transport, as well as being taken up with other national administrative tasks. On occasions, though not during the month in question, these duties had taken him overseas, sometimes on duties that were rather more showing the flag than doing or debating much in the way of serious policing matters.

The formal side of overseas visits rarely took much time, but they were always accompanied by receptions, dinners and, as often as not, various visits to the opera or other concerts. In June 1949, for example, he took greetings from the British Police to the Austrian Gendarmerie then celebrating its centenary. Since he had played such a key role in reorganising the policing of Vienna he was a logical choice. The reasons why he, together with Arthur Young, was selected to represent the British Police at the jubilee celebrations of the Antwerp Police two years later were much less apparent. Wilcox and Young were happy to travel together. They had, after all, worked together in Italy and as well as reminiscing they were able to talk about contemporary police issues; Young was now Commissioner of the City of London Police. They had no objection to paying their own fares, but they were a little taken aback when they found that they were expected to pay for a wreath to lay at the ceremony on behalf of all the Chief Constables in England and Wales. This expense was more than made up for, however, by the accommodation and the liberal supplies of drinks at almost every pause before, during and after formal proceedings. The two came away with a succession of humorous stories which may well have become a little embellished in the telling. Wilcox and Young were both tall men, and they had a smile about the Luxembourg representative who, in Wilcox's estimation, was about 5 feet 4 inches and weighed 18 stone. Presumably because of their height and build, Wilcox and Young were put in the front rank of the procession, but then they suddenly found themselves forced back by the insertion of a group of standard bearers between them and the band. They had to reduce their normal pace so as not to march into the standard bearers and the band – not to mention leaving the unfortunate Luxembourger puffing in the rear. There was also the problem that, until they heard it played for the third time or thereabouts, neither of them knew the Belgium national anthem or what they were supposed to do.

At the beginning of the 1960s Wilcox was invited to visit Italy for two weeks as one of three Chief Constables travelling with three county officials as representatives of the county and municipal associations. In his estimation, 'the most testing part' of the visit was getting through the succession of lunches and dinners. It was interesting to visit the headquarters of the Carabinieri as well as the greatly-expanded forensic science laboratories, both of which he had last seen about fifteen years earlier. Moreover, determined to get something positive from the visit, he made the most of his meeting with officers of the *Polizia Stradale*. These men were responsible for patrolling the Milan-Bologna section of the new autostrada that was planned to run south to Naples; he wanted to learn about their experience and practices to make comparisons with the recently opened M1 in his own jurisdiction. On his return he wrote his findings up in an article for the *County Councils' Gazette*, parts of which reappeared in the *Police Review*. This at least, he believed, provided some justification for his participation in the visit.

Rather more directly focussed on Wilcox's policing role were the meetings of the International Criminal Police Organisation, INTERPOL. This organisation had been established in Vienna in 1923 but taken over and used to their advantage by the Nazis. It was revised in 1946 and, while not involved directly in its restoration, the British always sent a delegation to its meetings, led by an Assistant Commissioner of the Metropolitan Police, and were active in its work. In 1965 Jean Nepote, a Frenchman who had been instrumental in re-establishing INTERPOL 20 years earlier, suggested to Wilcox that he propose either the Malaysian or the Thai delegates to stand for election as chair of a committee that was planned to investigate the protection of goods in transit. Nepote had tried hard and successfully to get the participation of countries from beyond Europe, but he was concerned that the annual conference was still dominated by Europeans. Wilcox was happy to help. He asked the Thai, who politely declined; so too did the Malaysian, who then went on to nominate Wilcox. A seconder promptly spoke up and Wilcox inadvertently found himself acting as chair of a committee that eventually produced eight papers.

Foreign tasks (and foreign junkets) took up only a fraction of the time drawing Wilcox away from what he considered to be his duties in Herts, specifically visiting police stations and talking to his officers, especially the beat constables and their new, motorised equivalents. He found himself spending hours in London taking to people from the Home Office and other ministries. There were eight Home Secretaries and three Permanent Under Secretaries with whom he had to deal at the Home Office during his 22 years in Herts. Each was very different; some were in post for a short period and had interests that were far from police and policing. Chuter Ede he thought 'dour.' Jim Callaghan came to the post with some knowledge of police and policing, but advising the Police Federation for the Royal Commission of 1960-62, when there was a Tory government, was rather different from acting as a Labour Home Secretary and being, at least in part, responsible for what could and what could not be afforded. Wilcox found Roy Jenkins to be zealous about reforming the police, though it would appear that at times he had little desire to consult at any length with senior officers. Rab Butler was, to Wilcox's mind, 'the most impressive', though this may have been rather more because of his cultural awareness rather than political awareness. When Butler came to open a new police station in Stevenage he commented on the unusual design of the newly-built church of St. Andrew and St. George. Wilcox told him that the locals described it as resembling an aircraft hanger, to which Butler pointed out that Lord Mottistone, a leading church architect who had been responsible for the design, was a personal friend and, on his request, the whole assemblage of the S.J.C., the chair of the Stevenage Development Corporation and various other officials then had to cross the road to inspect the church. Unfortunately for Butler, his tenure as Home Secretary was complicated by the clash between the Nottingham Watch Committee and its Chief Constable, Athelstan Popkess, and a succession of scandals over police behaviour towards members of the public. These latter prompted the Royal Commission which, while it also investigated recruitment and pay, was established primarily to consider the constitutional position of the police and specifically how they should be controlled and, if necessary, brought to account for any wrong-doing or exceeding their authority.

Wilcox was in sympathy with many of the Royal Commission's recommendations and had been pressing similar matters as best he could in Herts. In an interim report of November 1960, just ten months after it had been established, the Commission addressed the question of pay and the shortage of manpower in a period of rising crime. It proposed a pay formula that would increase the wage of a constable at the top of his scale by 40 per cent. The Treasury and the local authorities that would have to find the money seem to have thought that they were being bounced into making the award, but given the force of the case presented they felt that they had to agree to the increase. Yet as far as the Home Office was concerned, it promised the recruitment benefits that it wanted.

Wilcox had long fretted about the educational attainments of those coming forward as recruits and once again the Royal Commission was in agreement. That said, however, since shortly after the war things had begun to move nationally, again with a project that drew Wilcox away from Herts.

A police college, established in 1948, had seen 3,000 officers pass through its doors by 1960 and Wilcox was appointed as a member of the college's Advisory Board, whose task it was to suggest resources and improvements to the Commandant. He was not particularly happy with the way in which the college began; he did not advocate a new Hendon on Trenchard's lines, but he wanted to see bright young officers given the opportunity of rapid advancement. The first students had been selected for their past achievements rather than their promise; initially, the youngest was 37-years-old, and they were all established sergeants and inspectors.

Tangentially, it is interesting to note who was selected by the Home Office for the post of Commandant. Before the war there had been a significant number of former Army officers of field rank, especially among those appointed to command the county forces. After the war, there were also a large number of men with field rank commanding forces in both boroughs and counties, but these were usually police officers like Wilcox, Young and St. Johnston, who had gone into the Army during the war-time emergency. Many were Hendon men and they had earned their military rank because of the war.

When Trenchard appointed his first Commandant at Hendon he chose an Army man, Halland, but one with considerable police experience. The first Commandant at the post-war college at Ryton-on-Dunsmore, however, was a brigadier; the second was a Major-General, and neither had any police experience. Senior police officers particularly resented this; the appointment of a soldier was, after all, a job denied to a police officer. Since so much policing at the top level is administrative in character, it cannot be beyond challenge that senior Army experience was irrelevant, or that military officers were incapable of gaining and maintaining the confidence of their police authorities.

Men like Wilcox were qualified as much by their war experience as their training at Hendon. Yet Wilcox was opposed to soldiers as Commandants of the college, possibly because of his firmly-held belief that soldiers and police officers were trained to act and to think in quite different ways. As the major-general's retirement approached, Wilcox, together with Ronald (Ronnie) Wilson, the Chief Constable of West Sussex, met with senior figures in the Home Office to persuade them to install a serving police officer as Commandant. They were successful, and thereafter the Commandant always came from the police.

There was considerable debate in the Royal Commission about establishing a nation-wide detective force and a traffic corps, and indeed whether all of the separate local forces should be amalgamated into a single national police. Wilcox and other Chief Constables were strongly opposed to any of this. They shared the traditional view that a national force could, potentially, be directed by a government minister; and a little more than twenty years later Wilcox felt himself vindicated when, during the miners' strike of 1984-85, the House of Commons agreed that in such circumstances it was unacceptable to have such a national police. Yet at the time of the Royal Commission, Wilcox believed that the Commissioners were not particularly enthusiastic about recommending the continuation of local forces, and there was a powerfully-argued memorandum of dissent by A.L. Goodhart, Professor Emeritus of Jurisprudence and Master of University College, Oxford.

Goodhart's memorandum was widely-read and highly-praised. There had been successful amalgamations before, most notably in the immediate aftermath of the war, when around 60 of the smaller forces had been swallowed up by their larger neighbours. After the Labour Party won the 1964 election and Roy Jenkins became Home Secretary in late 1965, he used the enhanced powers provided him by the Police Act of the previous year to embark on an ambitious programme of police amalgamations.

Wilcox believed that Jenkins's plans smacked of being worked out by feeding statistics into a computer without any consideration of local feelings and with no consultation of the police or of local authorities. The scheme planned to reduce the number of forces from 125 to around 40, and had produced some amalgamations that he considered 'grotesque', such as the formation of the Devon and Cornwall Constabulary, when the distance from Land's End to the eastern border of Devon was greater than that from the latter to London, and the 'ill-conceived' unification of all the forces in Bucks, Berks and Oxfordshire into the Thames Valley Police. These survived, but some of the others, like the Mid-Anglian Constabulary, lasted only for relatively brief periods.

Wilcox was fortunate in that Hertfordshire survived untouched, but he found himself in a difficult position when Buckinghamshire County Council wrote to him with a request that, since he had been an Assistant Chief Constable in their county, he give evidence on their behalf before an Inquiry. Wilcox felt that he had to decline the request, however, since he had recently been appointed as President of the Association of Chief Police Officers (A.C.P.O.) and he feared that it might appear that he was speaking with their authority; and fortuitously this meant that he did not have to cross swords with an old friend, John McKay, another Hendon graduate and veteran of the Allied Military Governments in Italy and Austria. McKay was now an Inspector of Constabulary and it was his task to present the government's case that the amalgamations would lead to increased efficiency. There were other occasions, including issues arising from the amalgamations, when Wilcox was called upon to act and speak up on behalf of the police with A.C.P.O. backing.

It would probably be wrong to accuse the Home Office of ignoring the fact that a number of senior officers would be affected by the amalgamations, but such matters appeared to be a long way down the agenda; and while class divisions were declining, there were senior police officers who could be prickly and self-important. The social divisions between senior officers had begun to disappear in the inter-war period, especially as the Home Office began to insist that Chief Constables needed to have some knowledge of policing and that those in the counties needed to be a little more than simply gentlemen who fitted in with the county elite.

Nevertheless, when Wilcox returned from the war the Chief Constable of Lancashire preferred to wear plain clothes if he knew that he would be appearing alongside borough chiefs whose uniform had the same insignia as his own, but whose forces might amount to as few as 25 officers. There were also two distinct associations, one for county chiefs and one for those of the boroughs. The latter's annual conference heard talks on matters of practical policing throughout the inter-war years; the former saw itself rather more as a gentlemen's club. At one of the first meetings of the county association that he attended, Wilcox heard someone speak up for a fusion of the two associations. Wilcox also spoke in favour; after all, many of his war-time comrades were now in command of big cities. It soon became apparent that this was not something that a new boy should have done, and most of the old members appeared more than happy with the way that things were. The arguments of the few like Wilcox were listened to with impatience; but there was no vote and the chair passed on rapidly to the next business.

A degree of fusion was forced by the Oaksey Commission, which required hearing representatives of all Chief Constables together and not men sent from two distinct bodies; out of this came A.C.P.O., though initially the two distinct associations remained within it, each with its own president and secretary.

In 1956 Wilcox's old friend from Hendon days, Joe Simpson, transferred from being the Chief Constable of Surrey to an Assistant Commissioner of the Metropolitan Police; on his move he persuaded Wilcox to take over as secretary of the county conference – after all, he reasoned, the Herts headquarters in Hertford was about the same distance from London as was the Surrey headquarters in Guildford. Only after Wilcox had agreed to the post did he discover that would mean acting on behalf of all Chief Constables; this was another onerous task involving regular meetings with the Home Office and fronting concerns and issues on behalf of the police in both boroughs and counties. Yet by the time that the issue arose of what to do with senior officers surplus to requirements because of amalgamations, he already had experience of discussing the financial matters of Chief Constables with the Home Office.

As secretary, Wilcox found himself working alongside Norman Goodchild, the Chief Constable of Wolverhampton, on police pay rates. Their position was complicated. Pay negotiations were conducted by the Police Council for Great Britain, which was divided into three panels: the first panel was concerned with the Federated ranks, in other words the men of the lower ranks who were automatically members of the Police Federation; the second concerned those of the rank of superintendent; the third dealt with Chief Constables and their assistants. Wilcox and Goodchild were advisors on the first two panels, but on the third they were the representatives of the staff side. Wilcox was relieved that Goodchild appeared to revel in statistical tables and could more than hold his own with the negotiators on the other side of the table during the discussions in the third panel; but the two of them were united in keeping the Chief Constables distinct from other local government officials.

A major problem when Wilcox first appeared at meetings of the third panel was that the pay of Chief Constables had slipped some way behind that of the senior officials in local government. The Police Council negotiators believed that the answer was to link Chief Constables' pay with that of these officials. Wilcox insisted that Chief Constables were not like these other individuals. A Chief Constable had to have an independent status, because his duties of maintaining order and enforcing the law were independent of the direction of local government committees. He also stressed that if the pay of a Chief Constable was linked with that of a senior local government officer, then the pay of subordinate ranks in the police would also become linked with that of local government clerks; yet here again he insisted that the police constable's role was quite different.

Wilcox and Goodchild put the options to A.C.P.O., most of whose members, many approaching retirement age, wanted a quick resolution rather than long, drawn-out negotiations around possible future advantages. Yet Wilcox and Goodchild did not slacken their demands, and eventually they succeeded in getting a satisfactory settlement. Wilcox insisted that Goodchild played the key role here, though this might have been his own modesty. Certainly A.C.P.O. saw them playing an equal role, and both were presented with a Georgian silver tea service at the 1961 annual conference.

In addition to this role involving the resolution of pay for all chief officers, Wilcox, together with John Peel, the Chief Constable of Essex who was then President of A.C.P.O., organised the financial settlement that dissuaded Athelstan Popkess from pressing his case against Nottingham City Council. The leading solicitor with whom Peel and Wilcox discussed the case was sure that Popkess would win, but he warned that Popkess's reputation, and that of others, would be damaged while much dirty linen would be washed in public. Popkess was keen to have his day in court; but in the end persuasion and the financial sum that he was offered was sufficient to settle the matter. Peel and Wilcox were relieved and considered the £275 paid to the solicitor out of A.C.P.O. funds to have been money well spent.

However, arguing with the Home Office about the future of redundant senior police officers was rather different to settling litigation between a tough ex-soldier and long-time police officer and his former employer.

The amalgamations that began during the mid-1960s led to the disappearance of around 80 police forces. There were some senior officers who were prepared to take early retirement or serve in a reduced rank, but there were also others who considered themselves much too far from pensionable age to be expected either to take it immediately or to wait some years for it. There were others that thought themselves too young to leave the police, but too old to look for some new kind of job. Others were simply unhappy about being asked to serve in a reduced rank; and in any case, there were insufficient positions of assistant Chief Constable to absorb all of those who wished to carry on serving, even in a reduced rank.

The discussions dragged on into 1967, when Wilcox became President of A.C.P.O. and when the association instructed him and the new secretary, Sandy Wilson, the Chief Constable of Worcestershire, to make a direct approach to the Home Secretary. Wilcox and Wilson pressed the case to a sympathetic minister, but heard nothing for six months; and then they got the good news that their requests for pensions on early retirement and temporary posts of assistant Chief Constable had been largely approved.

Not every committee on which he served, and which took him away from his duties in Hertfordshire, was the result of his position in A.C.P.O. Wilcox could never understand what prompted him to agree to serve on a Home Office Departmental Committee looking for improved ways of collecting and presenting criminal statistics. He was well aware of the fact that the standard range of criminal offences from abortion to wounding provided no guidance on, for example, the severity of any violent offence; a charge depended upon what the prosecution decided to label a particular incident and this might vary from one police force area to another. There was also the problem of the 'dark figure', specifically crimes that were never reported to the police and therefore left no paper trail, and hence no means of being incorporated into the annual statistics. Wilcox was also disappointed that most of the 43 witnesses appearing before the committee seemed more interested in serving the interests of the organisation that they represented rather than assisting the broader aims of the committee. The saving grace for Wilcox was the fact that it enabled him to meet several outside experts brought in from universities to sit alongside Home Office statisticians. He also offered the headquarters staff of his own force to experiment with new methods of coding and punching record cards.

Eventually, as Roy Jenkins began to show impatience, a report was rushed out of just over 40 pages with additional appendices; but, Wilcox believed, it appeared only to be 'decently buried' in the Home Office archives.

A.C.P.O. work and Home Office committees were bureaucratic parts of the job which had to be done; they were invariably hard, time-consuming work and often difficult to get enthusiastic about. Wilcox's appointment as Regional Police Commander for the East of England in case of nuclear war was potentially the most bleak of his official appointments. He spent much time in an underground bunker near Cambridge preparing for the devastation and any flood of refugees and homeless people wandering the country having survived a nuclear strike. In his memoir he recalled driving back to his headquarters in Hatfield with 'an overwhelming feeling of the futility of the plans we had been making.' The one bright spot here was an annual exercise, held for three weeks every year, of a police mobile column. There was never any shortage of volunteers, who enjoyed the break from their normal duties to work in the convoy, maintain vehicles, use the radios and even to set up camp and cook. Wilcox took care to ensure that there was always plenty of food and drink.

The Police Dependents' Fund was altogether different from the meeting room and the nuclear bunker, and Wilcox found nothing futile or bleak in his work here. In the immediate aftermath of the murder of three Metropolitan detectives by Harry Roberts and two accomplices in August 1966, the Home Office received an anonymous donation of £100,000 for a trust that would help the families of officers killed or injured on duty.[6] Lord Stonham, the Minister of State at the Home Office, contacted Wilcox's old friend from Hendon, Joe Simpson, who was now the Metropolitan Police Commissioner. Simpson in turn contacted Wilcox and discussed the creation of the trust with him; as well as their long-standing friendship, Simpson was well aware of the role that Herts Police had played in Roberts's arrest. Together they resisted Stonham's suggestion that a management committee for the trust should be chaired by a Home Office civil servant. Wilcox pointed to the National Police Fund (N.P.F.) – a 'closed' fund - to which people had subscribed in the aftermath of the General Strike, and which had been required to preserve its capital and distribute only its income.

---

6 The anonymous donor was later revealed to be Billy Butlin, who had made his name and fortune through holiday camps.

Restrictions on investment policy and inflation had eroded value, and the Fund had been unable to respond in a sufficiently flexible way to deal with compensation issues. It is not entirely clear that he understood the legal and financial niceties of the N.P.F., but he was determined that the restrictions which limited its payments should not apply to the new Police Dependents' Trust.

The Home Office accepted this advice, and the new trust was established on a different, more flexible basis. While he probably did not have the idea in mind, Wilcox's reward was to be elected as chairman at the first meeting of the management committee. The committee itself was made up of a representative from every rank in the service, a police pensioner and a police widow; the Home Office provided the secretary. It met every month, usually over two successive days, and set about spending immediately. During its first year, it spent more than the amount originally invested by the trustees, but a steady trickle of donations kept the Fund solvent. Wilcox never ceased to be moved by the regular receipt of letters from those who were helped.

In the aftermath of the Second World War, 22 years was a long time to serve in the same place as a Chief Constable, but Wilcox never showed any inclination to move. Especially he showed no interest in moving back to the Metropolitan Police like many of his fellow students from Hendon.

Looking back, he believed that he had been sounded out on two occasions. Joe Simpson, when a deputy at the Metropolitan Police, unexpectedly took him out to lunch one day, mentioned that there would soon be a vacancy in the rank of Assistant Commissioner and that the Home Secretary was keen to bring in a senior officer from the provinces. But Wilcox always considered that the Commissioner had the Home Secretary constantly breathing down his neck and, in consequence, he had less freedom for manoeuvre than a provincial chief. This was probably a mistaken belief, since senior civil servants responsible for the police seem to have found it difficult to get the Home Secretary's attention and regarded the Home Office as not a particularly effective police authority for London. But Wilcox was fixed in his belief that politicians should not have any role in policing. As noted earlier, he was keen to have his Police Headquarters in Welwyn since it kept him at some distance from County Hall and local politicians in Hertford.

The second occasion when he thought that possibly he was being looked at for a post in the Metropolitan Police came a few years later, when he and five other provincial Chief Constables were invited to have lunch at the Hyde Park Hotel with the new Home Secretary Roy Jenkins, his Under Secretary and the Permanent Under Secretary. Though neither he nor any of the other senior officers knew why they had been invited, Wilcox later thought that it was as good a method of interviewing as any other. Shortly afterwards one of the invitees was announced as an Assistant Commissioner. This was Robert Mark, who went on to be Commissioner. Mark was coolly received in his new post like Arthur Young before him; this appears to have been because he came from the provinces, but by now it seems that, in addition, there was also a Hendon clan dominating senior posts in the Metropolitan Police. As far as Mark was concerned, it was far better facing this coolness than having to take a subordinate rank given that his Leicester City force was soon to be amalgamated with Leicestershire.

Probably, Wilcox would not have faced these problems; he was, after all a Hendon graduate and he had served in the Metropolitan Police, but he enjoyed doing what he did and where he did it. Perhaps too, deep down, his Italian experience had left a mark on him; towards the end of 1944 he had written to Ethel about his wish to be the Chief Constable of a county. He knew that if he returned to the Metropolitan Police he would be an 'assistant' or 'deputy' before he had any chance of becoming commissioner. He had experience of being a deputy in Italy, and of being continually passed over for the top job, even when he knew that the new superior could not do the job as well as him.

Wilcox's twenty-second year in Hertfordshire coincided with his 60th birthday, and he appears to have thought that he really ought to retire at this point and hand over to a younger man. There had been an enormous number of changes in police and policing during the quarter of a century since the end of the war. A new, younger Chief Constable would be more in tune with these changes, and would bring fresh ideas moulded in recent experience and awareness of the way that society was changing; it was only right, he believed, for someone of his age to stand down.

But Wilcox was still physically fit and mentally active; his children had grown up and all he had to do was to find something to keep him busy.

CHAPTER 8

RETIREMENT

Still a Busy Life

Wilcox had made no plans about what to do when he retired; however, for the next 15 years or so he kept busy engaging in various committees and enquiries. Both surprising and exhilarating for him, however, was the invitation to engage in academic work. While engaged with the Home Office's Departmental Inquiry into improving the collection and presentation of criminal statistics, Wilcox had met the influential criminologist Leon Radzinowicz.

Born in Poland, Radzinowicz had been in England since 1938. In 1949 he became director of the Department of Criminal Science at the University of Cambridge; ten years later he established the university's Institute of Criminology. Wilcox had been forced to leave school with few qualifications, but Radzinowicz encouraged him to develop his academic interests. Within a year of retirement, Wilcox had applied for, and received, one of the new Cropwood Fellowships offered by the Institute.

For several months in 1970 he spent the weekdays in Cambridge, returning to the family home in Harpenden at weekends. He soaked up the atmosphere of the university; he wandered the streets, the colleges, the Backs and the churches. He also found himself invited to dine at high tables, renewing his acquaintance with Rab (now Lord) Butler, who had been Master of Trinity College since his elevation to the peerage and departure from politics five years earlier. Wilcox thought how much he had aged since they had last met. Yet in spite of the relaxation provided by the groves of academe, Wilcox never forgot why he was there and he produced a manuscript which he called 'Enforcing the Law with Discretion.' The focus of the manuscript was the role of discretionary power used by the police in deciding whether or not to prosecute, an important topic that very few had addressed before. Butterworths, a well-known legal publisher, changed the title to the rather more catchy *The Decision to Prosecute* and brought the book out to considerable praise in the summer of 1972. An evaluation of the Cropwood Fellowships conducted in 2009 singled the book out as one of those emanating from the overall programme that 'made fundamental and lasting contributions to both academic and professional knowledge in their respective fields.'

While he was at Cambridge, Wilcox was invited by the Home Secretary to serve as a member of the Parole Board for England and Wales. The three years of his appointment were to consume an enormous amount of his time The Board had been created in 1968 following the Criminal Justice Act of the previous year; its remit was to assess the risk to the public of prisoners requesting release on parole. As a non-departmental public body, it carried out its work at arm's length of the Home Office and while the Home Secretary could veto any recommendation for release, he could not overturn any decision to refuse parole.

The Chairman of the Board was Lord Hunt, a former distinguished Army officer who had also led the 1953 expedition that finally conquered Mount Everest. While the invitation to join the board came from the Home Office, Hunt stressed to Wilcox that he needed men like him to develop a closer relationship with the police. The other members of the board were a cross-section of lawyers, academics, doctors and officials from the probation and welfare services. Most of these still were still working, and consequently it fell to retired members, like Wilcox, to make most of the visits to prisons and, in Wilcox's case, also to various police headquarters.

In addition to these visits there were the meetings that decided on whether or not an individual was likely to lead an honest life if granted parole. Each meeting required reading and mastering of dossiers prepared by individuals who had knowledge of the offender from the police that arrested him (or her), from prison officers, doctors and others. Wilcox confessed that on many occasions he changed the view that he had gained from reading of the dossiers when he heard the arguments presented and debated by the panel; though he also always felt that due weight had to be given to the gravity of the offence. He also developed a more critical view of the system during his time on the Board. While he felt that prison, probation and welfare officers worked hard to prepare prisoners for leaving prison and for what they would experience on the outside, talking with prisoners showed him that they viewed the system in a very different light. In particular, the prisoners appeared largely unconcerned about the conditions surrounding their parole and, particularly, with the fact that they could be recalled for breaking its terms. Moreover, it seemed to Wilcox that the prisoners were right; the supervision was generally negligible, and very little notice seemed to be taken of repeated breaches of their licence.

While Wilcox busied himself with academic pursuits and committee work, a number of his police acquaintances and friends joined new and expanding security companies on retirement. The most notable of these was Securicor, which had its origins in the mid-1930s and which had become a leading security business in the post-war period. The management of the company seems to have assumed that Wilcox would be delighted to work for them, if only in a part-time capacity. But he had little remaining interest in advising and organising the protection of goods and valuables in transit. He felt that he was giving that up when he left the police, and had no enthusiasm for picking up a similar harness, no matter how remunerative.

A few years later he found himself involved on the fringe of Securicor, but in rather different circumstances.

Lord Wigg had never held high office in the Labour party, but he was close to Harold Wilson. In 1967 he had entered the House of Lords and, at the same time, he became Chair of the Horserace Betting Levy Board. Securicor had the responsibility for protecting racecourses, but its guards were reported as being poorly-trained and lacking in supervision, while the company itself did not seem particularly keen to continue its commitment to the job. Wigg asked Wilcox for his opinion on a report prepared by a Superintendent in the Lancashire Constabulary and for any suggestions on how matters might be improved, and Wilcox suggested that the Board should have its own security body. This chimed with Wigg's own ideas, and he promptly asked Wilcox if he would be prepared to lead it. Again Wilcox declined; while Wigg was a great fan of horse racing, Wilcox took no interest. He pointed out to Wigg that he had never placed a bet in his life and had never been to a racecourse other than putting in an appearance as Chief Constable at point-to-point races in Herts. In addition, he feared that the work of such a post would necessitate him giving up his position on the Parole Board which, while time-consuming, he found satisfying and enjoyed. Perhaps the fact that he was not intending to take on the leadership of any new security body eased the acceptance of his ideas when presented to a very frosty meeting that involved the Senior Steward of the Jockey Club, always jealous of outsiders becoming involved in their proceedings, and a member of the Horseracing Anti-Doping Committee. In the end Wigg got his way with a new policing body, and Wilcox got his way with not having to manage it.

The academic world continued to draw on Wilcox's expertise and his interest. In 1972 he was invited to join the editorial board of *Criminal Law Review* and delighted in making occasional contributions. Although initially reluctant, he agreed to act as an assessor on a project run by the Institute of Judicial Administration at the University of Birmingham. The aim of the project was to explore why half of the individuals who entered a plea of 'not guilty' were acquitted by a jury. Was it that too many innocent people were being prosecuted? The methodology of the research was for a group of research workers to collect a thousand sets of committal papers, that is the depositions on which a prosecution relied, and then to have two assessors predict the probable outcome. The predictions were then to be checked against the actual verdicts. Wilcox's initial reservations concerned the absence of defence evidence, of seeing the defendants and witnesses cross-examined in court. He was persuaded to participate by the researchers, who argued that it would be highly beneficial to have a sceptic among the assessors.

Again the work was hard and time-consuming. Wilcox and his fellow assessor, Dr. J.P. Wilson, a former Clerk to the Justices in Sunderland and editor of *Stone's Justices Manual*, worked alone at their homes without consultation, but significantly predicted the outcome of the trials correctly in five out of six cases. The researchers were, in consequence, able to conclude that weak cases could be identified by a stricter examination of the evidence at the committal stage. It also emerged that a high proportion of acquittals were directed by judges on legal grounds without the verdict being left to juries; but it did not deflect Wilcox from his belief that many acquittals were the result of the rules of evidence which excluded relevant facts from being passed to juries for consideration before their verdict.

While he was working on the Birmingham project Wilcox received a letter from the Home Office asking if he would be interested in accepting a fellowship from the Council of Europe to study the prosecution process. He agreed, but heard nothing for six months. When he asked the Home Office what had happened they passed the buck to the Council of Europe, but eventually the fellowship came through and Wilcox set off for Strasbourg where he found himself part of a group of four; the others were a senior French lawyer, a German academic and a Swedish civil servant from the Swedish equivalent of the Home Office. Their task was to report on prosecuting practice across the 18 countries that were members of the Council, but at their first meeting the full title of their investigation gave Wilcox some difficulties.

The Council wanted a report on 'prosecuting practice [as] governed by the opportunity principle' and he did not know what was meant by the 'opportunity principle.' It was explained that, in European legal practice, there were opposing principles – that of legality, by which the law had always to be enforced, and that of opportunity, which meant that prosecution would not be justified in exceptional circumstances.

Wilcox took this to mean that they were expected to investigate the use of discretion in enforcing the criminal law, a topic with which he felt at home. The problem of collecting data, however, was extremely difficult. The four of them found that the only way that they could cover all 18 countries in the Council was by using a questionnaire, but as these came back it was apparent that no-one was prepared to give much information and that such as they did give was essentially a statement of the regulations without any discussion of any difficulties or comment on how these functioned in practice or whether they might be improved. Wilcox was given responsibility for exploring the way in which matters worked in England and Wales, Scotland, Northern Ireland and the Republic of Ireland. He took the topic seriously and, since the European funds would not run to it, he paid for himself to visit the Directors of Public Prosecutions in London, Belfast and Dublin and the Crown Agent in Edinburgh. All of them, as well as the police with whom he spoke were helpful. He prepared his report, and sent it to each of the interviewees to ensure that there was nothing to which they objected.

The group met four times in Strasbourg. Each meeting lasted for three days and all went reasonably well until the final meeting. The secretary, who Wilcox had assumed would write the final report, explained that this was not his job, and there was little agreement on what rules should govern prosecutors in the exercise of discretion. The German sociologist wanted them to be guided by movements for social reform; the Swede was in favour of diverting people from the criminal courts to welfare agencies; the French lawyer wanted to ensure that prosecutors and judges should be protected from government interference; and Wilcox felt that there was little point in making any recommendations since, while perhaps a dozen

European countries might find any recommendations acceptable, there was no chance that such acceptance would be found in the British Isles. Eventually it was decided that each member of the group would submit his own report. The Secretariat did not approve, though went ahead with the four separate reports. The Council of Ministers was even less pleased. They had wanted unanimous recommendations which would enable them to pass a resolution urging all of the 18 nations to adopt a uniform pattern, not a series of statements emphasising that there were a series of different legal systems and traditions which made harmonisation unlikely, if not impossible.

Wilcox was always wary of sections of the criminal justice system coming under government control, and he always opposed anything that had the potential to weaken the independence of the police or the courts. This was a traditional element within the perception of the unique nature of the English/British police – it was non-political. Wilcox had shown his concerns about such matters in the continuing existence of the political police in Austria. On the parochial level in England he had kept his headquarters away from the local politicians in the county hall in Hertford; and on the national level, particularly when he held senior positions in A.C.P.O., he had spoken out against anything that might have provided an opportunity for ministerial involvement in the British police. The police, he believed, should be allowed to get on with policing; they knew what the problems were and the best reforms in policing were organic, such as the development of the first juvenile liaison system in Liverpool and Popkess's creation of civilian traffic wardens in Nottingham. Politicians, it seemed to Wilcox, had a bad habit of jumping in to resolve a problem with new legislation, which was invariably unnecessary and which invariably created new problems that the police had to sort out.

The proposal for a Crown Prosecution Service that emerged from the 1981 report of the Royal Commission on Criminal Procedure was a case in point. This meant taking the prosecution away from the police who had investigated an offence, even though technically police officers prosecuted as private citizens. In place of the police a central body would make the decision of whether to prosecute, and although the judicial system had been moving towards such a body for many years, Wilcox was worried about giving these decisions to a centralised organisation. He wrote an article for the *Criminal Law Review* suggesting that it might be better to have local committees, rather like the police committees, making these decisions. When he was asked by the Medico-Legal Society to speak in their 1982 programme, he decided to draw on his experience with the Council of Europe and proposed the title 'Criminal investigation in the hands of lawyers.'

As he began collecting notes for this talk he became slightly alarmed by how little he actually knew about the situation across Europe. He was fortunate in being able to call on the assistance of the son of the secretary of the group with which he had worked in Strasbourg. The son had followed his father into the legal profession, and was working as a public prosecutor in Paris.

Wilcox, in turn, called on the assistance of his eldest daughter. Susan had been called to the Bar at Gray's Inn almost exactly 30 years after her father, though eventually she found the career a little too chancy. In this instance, however, she travelled with him to France and helped him with his French in general and with technical legal terms in particular. If she had hoped for some kind of holiday, she was soon disabused and appears to have spent lunch hours both trying to eat and trying to explain legal intricacies.

He also followed up contacts in the French *Police Judiciaire*, the detective branch, who had far more freedom to act on their own initiative than he had expected. Both of them were shocked when they sat in on the trial of two Black Africans accused of a mugging. Neither of them felt that there was any case to answer, but the accused's defence was rejected and the two unfortunate men were both given two years' imprisonment. Wilcox, thinking in the English terms of Judges' Rules, asked the magistrate what he would do if he thought the police had obtained information by ill-treatment. 'The rather baffled magistrate,' Susan recalled, 'after a few moments of thought, replied that if it was a glaring case he might have a quiet word with a senior police officer.' Wilcox did not pass on this vignette in his presentation to the Medico-Legal Society.

In his recollections, and no doubt with his usual modesty, he stated that he was unsure how his paper had gone down with the Society. But there were a large number of questions, as is evidenced by the printed version of the paper. The questions, it seems, lasted longer than the paper, the president having to bring the proceedings to an end and the printed report concludes with '(Hearty Applause)'.

At the beginning of 1977 Wilcox was asked by the Home Office to act as an assessor alongside Patrick Bennett Q.C. at a tribunal involving a senior police officer. The accusations against the officer were not greatly dissimilar from, but rather more serious than, those against his first Chief Constable in Bristol.

Stanley Parr, the Chief Constable of Lancashire was reported to have made improper use of police drivers and transport, and to have abused his powers in favour of personal friends, some of whom appear to have been rather undesirable and not the kind of people with whom a senior policeman should mix.

Sir Douglas Osmond, the Chief Constable of Hampshire and another Hendon graduate who had served as Halland's personal staff officer in occupied Germany, conducted an investigation which he presented to the Home Office, the D.P.P. and the Lancashire Police Authority at the end of December 1976. The Clerk of the Police Authority passed the report to the Chairman who sharply criticised Osmond's report; several new members of the authority were not shown the report and a cover-up looked to be planned. Over a period of two weeks, a tribunal was held in Preston with leading counsel representing both sides. It was held in secret and well away from the press; Bennett and Wilcox were whisked away about 15 miles each evening to Southport. They upheld Osmond's findings, and Parr was dismissed.

A sour note for Wilcox to end his links with the police perhaps, but it contributed significantly to the fact that in future, officers of A.C.P.O. rank were not regularly appointed internally.

Slowing Down

There comes a time when age catches up with everyone, even those who live beyond their allotted three-score-years-and-ten. Wilcox liked to keep active. He went swimming every morning for as long as he was able. He took a keen interest in what was going on in matters of crime, penal policy and policing.

Approaching the age of ninety, he had a letter published in *The Independent* expressing concern about the creation of an officer class on an Army model for the police:

> A police officer must act on his own initiative, using his own discretion. He is answerable to the law for his actions. It is therefore essential that senior police officers should themselves in their early years have the experience of dealing with all classes of society. This hard-won experience enables them to understand the problems and difficulties of those in the junior ranks whom they have to guide and encourage.

This echoed the point that he had made with reference to the Commandant of the police college a Ryton-on-Dunsmore, and was open to the same sort of challenge. At the top level much policing was administrative in character, and this was something that Wilcox had done well. Moreover, he had gained enormous experience in this area as a result of his wartime career.

As the years passed he became frustrated by an increasing deafness that prevented him from appreciating music and the tapes that he enjoyed with poems and speeches read by the likes of Lord Olivier and Sir John Gielgud.

In August 1993, Stephen took him on holiday to Brittany. Wilcox had a wonderful time, but was relieved to be able to leave everything to his son, though there was little that Stephen could do about one bed and breakfast in which they stayed which could not cope with Wilcox's height. The bed was too small, and the wash-basin and mirror were such that he had to shave while on his knees. In a short account of the trip he wrote of how it brought home that he was 'in need of a minder':

> Long, long ago I was capable of driving on the continent. Not now.

> Getting a car on and off a ferry would be too much for me. Finding my way about the decks, using the lifts, locating the cabin, and queuing for meals – even using the machine that pours out a cup of coffee as you push the tray along in the self service – finds me helpless. As for putting in a telephone call from a kiosk to England it is a feat I would never attempt.

He may not have had a minder, but he had Ethel who was still lively and still going strong. In the interview that she gave at the turn of the millennium, she spoke of his kindness, especially to members of the family less fortunate than themselves; of the way that he was always there for the children. One reason for their long life together, she believed, was that neither of them had a temper and neither ever raised a voice to the other.

Reading, which had always been his main hobby, and hearing what his children were doing, became Wilcox's way of passing time. Weather permitting he also enjoyed sitting in his garden during the evening with a glass of wine. He had attempted to put a veto on gifts for his 90th birthday, but Stephen ensured that, amongst other things, a mixed collection of Italian wine was sent to him. In a thank you letter Wilcox gently chided him for breaking the veto, adding that he intended to take his time drinking the wine 'first consulting the Wine Encyclopaedia and the Atlas of Wine to study the region where the vines are grown.' He already knew about the Lacrima Christie, he added; it grew on the slopes of Vesuvius and he remembered it from his time in Naples during the war. He also explained that he was intending to test his brain with a six-chapter story for his new grand-daughter.

He died on 8 February 2002. A family service was held at the local crematorium. It was organised and presided over by his children, who all spoke warmly and offered fond memories. 'A man of few words,' recalled Bridget, and with 'a sense of the ridiculous [who] hated pomposity.' A 'generous, fair and caring man' who set himself the highest standards, said Stephen, and 'who did his good deeds quietly and without fuss.' For Susan, he was a man of unquestionable but undemonstrative integrity, who Chaucer would have recognised as his 'parfit gentle knight.'

A.F. 'MICHAEL' WILCOX

TIMELINE

1909   (18 April) Born Bristol.

1924   Death of father forces him to leave school and go to work at H.Steadman & Co., boot and leggings manufacturers and shippers.

1929   (13 June) Joins Bristol City Police.

1934   (10 May) Enters Trenchard's Police College, Hendon.

1935   (26 July) Passes out of Hendon and posted to 'E' Division; 21 August 1936 to 'S Division; 1 November 1937 to C.I.D.; 29 November 1938 to 'P' Division as Station Inspector; 27 October 1941 to 'B' Division as Sub-Divisional Inspector.

1939   (22 December) Marries Ethel Wilmott (primary school teacher).

1940   Commended in case of housebreaking when off duty.

1941   Called to the Bar.
Daughter Susan born.

1943   Commended in case of keeping a disorderly house.
Daughter Bridget born.
(6 August) Temporary Commission as 2nd Lieutenant in Civil Affairs.
(11 August) Acting Major; lands first in Algeria, then on bridgehead at Salerno.
(December) Chief of Public Safety with American 5th Army.

1944   (4 March) Acting Lt. Col, on staff of Allied Commission for occupation of Rome, in charge of Public Safety Officers in Italy and linking with Italian ministries responsible for Police, Prisons and Fire Service.
(4 June 1944) Temporary Lt. Colonel – substantive Major.
(Christmas period) First leave since 1943. Looking for posts in English police forces.

1945   (January) Urged by Arthur Young applies for a post in the Allied Government of Austria.

(8 May) Ordered to Udine en route for Austria, then crosses border to Klagenfurt. When the four powers finally settle the division of Austria and Vienna the British Public Safety Branch destined for Vienna are ordered back to Udine to await final agreement of their passage to the city. Wilcox takes another leave so as to be interviewed by West Suffolk and the City of Liverpool (neither of which he is offered). Another brief period with his family.

(8 September) First meeting of the Public Safety Branches of the four powers with clear divisions apparent.

1946   (late summer) encouraged by Young, applies for and gets post of Assistant Chief Constable of Buckinghamshire. Authorised to keep title of Lieutenant Colonel on leaving Army.

1947   (12 February) interviewed for and get the post of Chief Constable of Hertfordshire; takes up the post on 1 April.

1948   Son Stephen born.

1969   Retires from Police.

1970   Cropwood Fellow, Institute of Criminology, University of Cambridge; invited by Home Secretary to join the Parole Board.

1972   Appointed to Editorial Board of Criminal Law Review; appointed assessor of project at University of Birmingham on 'not guilty' pleas; initial request from Home Secretary to sit on European Commission on differing prosecution processes across Europe (nothing done until 1973).

1977   One of two assessors investigating the findings of corrupt practices by the Chief Constable of Lancashire.

1982   Having agreed to speak to the Medico-Legal Society on the role of lawyers in European criminal investigations embarks on his own study in France.

1998   Grand-daughter born (to Stephen and his wife).

2002   (8 February) Died Harpenden.

REFERENCES

As mentioned in the Introduction, this book does not have footnotes or references to the documents quoted since the overwhelming majority remain uncatalogued in the hands of the Wilcox family. The references that are listed below provide the best route into the events and social context that formed the background to Wilcox's life.

Police history has become a major interest among social historians researching crime and criminal justice. T.A. Critchley, *A History of Police in England and Wales* (2nd edn. London: Constable, 1978) is the best of the histories in a Reithian mode. Critchley, a senior figure in the Home Office, concentrates on police legislation and administration. He knew Wilcox well, and was one of the many to send him hand-written congratulations when he was appointed C.B.E. in 1967. More recently, there are two books by Clive Emsley, *The English Police: A Political and Social History* (2nd. edn. London and Harlow: Longman, 1996) and *The Great British Bobby: A History of British Policing from the 18th Century to the Present* (revised edn. London: Quercus, 2009) which take a rather more critical line of Reith. Keith Laybourn and David Taylor, *Policing in England and Wales, 1918-39: The Fed, Flying Squads and Forensics* (Houndmills, Basingstoke: Palgrave Macmillan, 2011) is useful for Wilcox's early years in the police, but they do not discuss the Hendon scheme. The most useful assessment of Hendon and its subsequent impact is to be found in a few pages of Robert M. Morris, 'What the Met brought to the party – reinforcement, colonization, specialization and fusion', in Kim Stevenson, David J. Cox and Iain Channing, eds. *Leading the Police: A History of Chief Constables 1835-2017* (London: Routledge, 2018).

F.S.W. Donnison, *Civil Affairs and Military Government: Central Organisation and Planning* (London: H.M.S.O., 1961) is an official history of Civil Affairs in Europe during and shortly after the Second World War. C.R.S. Harris, *Allied Military Administration in Italy 1943-1945* (London: H.M.S.O., 1957) is similarly an official history, and focusses little on the experience of the men on the ground. J.R.H. Nott-Bower, *Public Safety Austria* (London; New Scotland Yard, 1947) is a little more forthcoming in this respect but, with the exception of the personal account of a P.S.O. based in a relatively typical part of Austria, it provides little discussion of the four-power relationship within Vienna, or within the country as a whole. Italy has been much better served as far as issues facing Allied officers on the ground with books such as Tim Newark, *The Mafia at War: Allied Collusion with the Mob* (London: Greenhill Books, 2007) which focusses rather more on the Americans than the British and Isobel Williams, *Allies and Italians under Occupation: Sicily and Southern Italy, 1943-45* (Houndmills, Basingstoke: Palgrave Macmillan, 2013). Jonathan Dunnage, *Mussolini's Policemen: Behaviour, Ideology and Institutional Culture in Representation and Practice* (Manchester: Manchester University Press, 2012) is valuable for outlining the police institutions with which Wilcox had to deal when he was responsible for policing in the Allied Military Government. It is also worth noting the excellent study by the novelist and travel writer Norman Lewis, who served as an intelligence officer in Italy, *Naples '44: An Intelligence Officer in the Italian Labyrinth* (Eland edn.: London, 1983). Austria and Vienna are much less well served, but see James Jay Carafano, *Waltzing into the Cold War: the Struggle for Occupied Austria* (College Station: Texas A & M University Press, 2002). While useful in many respects, Carafino concentrates on high politics and has little to say about policing. Jill Lewis, *Workers and Politics in Occupied Austria, 1945-55* (Manchester: Manchester

University Press, 2007) focuses on the issues much more from the point of view of the Austrians but, again, has little on the matters that occupied Wilcox and his Public Safety officers.

Clive Emsley, *Exporting British Policing During the Second World War: Policing Soldiers and Civilians* (London: Bloomsbury, 2017) looks as civilian police officers serving as Civil Affairs officers and as members of the S.I.B. in Europe throughout the wartime period; it gives the personal detail lacking in Donnison and Harris. His *Soldier, Sailor, Beggarman, Thief: Crime and the British Armed Services since 1914* (Oxford: Oxford University Press, 2013) looks at the offences committed by British service personnel and there is considerable material here on Italy during the Second World War.

Similarly, The National Archives at Kew appear to have much more information on Italy than on Austria. Particularly useful here as a way in is Arthur Young's manuscript 'Report on the Work of British Police Officers of Allied Military Government and Allied Commission in Italy' in WO 220/492, and much of this seems to have been taken from a report by John McKay, another Hendon graduate, who became Chief H.M.I. in 1970. A copy of McKay's manuscript is in the Wilcox family papers.

INDEX

Index

CPSIA information can be obtained
at www.ICGtesting.com
Printed in the USA
LVHW080317050319
609511LV00012B/52/P

9 781911 273622